Why Doctors Need This Book, by These Authors

Ike Devji. J.D.

The business of medicine, as well as the amount of time, effort and education required by doctors to keep and grow their personal wealth is more onerous than ever. This book provides a unique lay-out which equates to a primary care or "financial doctor" providing vital financial health information as well as the input of a variety of other specialists to deliver the required proactive legal and financial care most doctors require.

This book will be of tremendous value to both new doctors and those well established in their practice for many years. **Young doctors** will learn "healthy wealth habits" and be educated on specific strategies that will help build an efficient foundation for long term wealth and success with minimum effort and exposure. **Older doctors** will use this book as a check-up, to help diagnose and proactively treat any legal or financial ailments now, before the symptoms become chronic and while the opportunity to make a difference still exists.

There's an old saying, roughly paraphrased that says, "Success is a combination of who you know and the books you read." You are off to a very good start here. No book can fully address every issue or the differences that make every doctor, practice and family unique. We hope this book empowers you to ask questions, keep learning and reach out for experienced, personalized help.

OPTIMAL FINANCIAL HEALTH

OPTIMAL FINANCIAL HEALTH

The Doctor's Essential Wealth Management and Preservation Handbook

Anthony C. Williams, ChFC, RFC, CLU,
and Marc E. Ortega, ChFC, RFC

iUniverse, Inc.
Bloomington

Optimal Financial Health
The Doctor's Essential Wealth Management and Preservation Handbook

iUniverse books may be ordered through booksellers or by contacting:

iUniverse
1663 Liberty Drive
Bloomington, IN 47403
www.iuniverse.com
1-800-Authors (1-800-288-4677)

ISBN: 978-1-4759-2523-4 (sc)
ISBN: 978-1-4759-2525-8 (hc)
ISBN: 978-1-4759-2524-1 (ebk)

Library of Congress Control Number: 2012908984

Printed in the United States of America

iUniverse rev. date: 09/07/2012

CONTENTS

I: GETTING STARTED

II: GROW YOUR WEALTH

III: PROTECT YOUR WEALTH

IV: DISTRIBUTE YOUR WEALTH

V: ENJOY IT

VI: CONCLUSIONS

AUTHOR'S NOTE

As you likely notice, throughout the book, there are references to Being Lucky. In fact, there is a chapter saying, "What Is Luck?" You may be asking yourself, how does this fit? Well, our first book is titled, "Be One of the Lucky Ones A Specialty Doctors' Guide to Financial Freedom and Peace of Mind." This new book is an expansion of that book with significantly more material while including much of the original content. We felt a title change was necessary to adequately communicate the theme of this new book.

THANK YOU

A personal note of thanks goes to several people. Thanks to our clients who provided feedback and ultimately asked the question, "*Is there anything we can read about this stuff?*" Thank you to Sheila Evans, Bonita Mac Farland, and Maidi Terry for their input, formatting, and editing. Thank you to our mentors, without whom none of this would be possible. Thank you to our contributing authors for their content. Finally, huge thanks go to our wives. We realize we wouldn't be where we are if it not for the support and love of Wendy and Dee.

FOREWORD

Yes, I'm one of the lucky ones. I have it all. And no, I'm not independently wealthy or even in the top tax bracket. But I work in a field where I do something that I believe makes people's lives better. Let me explain.

Many people ask me what brought me back to the workforce when they find out that I went back to work after a three year maternity leave. At the time, I had a ten-month-old daughter and a two-year-old son. But, even with the joy and satisfaction I felt from raising my kids, I felt I was missing a part of myself. Anthony Williams had called me over the summer of 2007 and said he and Marc were writing this book and asked me if I would be willing to contribute as an editor.

During that process, I felt revitalized. The concepts of financial planning that Anthony and Marc were defining as their platform were being further refined and improved. They were truly becoming individuals with expertise in their field. When the phone call came from Anthony telling me they were almost ready to start their own firm, I was thrilled to hear what I was hoping he'd say: the only thing missing was me!

Since that time, I have assisted in bringing over our most valued clients, building a website, staffing an office, streamlining investment and insurance processing, data storage, and keeping up with FINRA compliance requirements. Most of all, I have watched as our practice has grown through referrals and positive word of mouth.

Some of our clients began with us years ago in the infant stages of medical residency. Now, they have built assets, wealth protection, and a source for referrals for everything from a contract review attorney to a mortgage broker. They have started on a journey towards their financial goals: a journey that will have unplanned stops and moments of uncertainty along with the pride and satisfaction that comes from watching their own progress. But ask any one of them, and I bet they will tell you that the smartest thing they ever did was simply to get started.

It might sound silly, but when I take care of a simple task for one of our clients, most of whom are busy doctors, I feel that I am empowering them to focus their energies and attention toward the things at which they excel as well as things they enjoy. And since a happy client rewards me as well as my firm, it's a win-win.

Of course, working for Anthony and Marc has its other perks. They both have families. When we all met, Marc was married, Anthony was engaged, and I was a newlywed. Now, we have four kids and four dogs between us. Our lives have become intertwined in the process of launching Mosaic Financial Associates. I had to consider this when I was asked to join them. I knew it was going to be more than a "job". It was my future and I wanted to be a part of it. I had to believe, down to my core, that I trusted their vision, expertise, as well as their spiritual and moral fortitude if I was going to attach my future to theirs.

As you can see, I made the choice to join them. And never, in my seven years of working with them, have I ever had one conversation that made me doubt their sole mission: their clients' total financial well-being. Trends have come and gone, the market has risen and fallen, and still our clients remain steadfast on their path to prosperity. To use a "medical metaphor" as we often do here, our continuing education keeps us abreast of all of the latest products, offerings, and investment vehicles much like a good doctor needs to stay knowledgeable of new treatments and procedures as they arise. At the same time, we are wary of fads and quick fixes. Just as a doctor would always be wise to prescribe good old-fashioned nutrition and exercise, we encourage discipline and "early intervention" in beginning savings and planning, following time-tested rules of financial planning as well.

My job is one of support: I support Marc and Anthony in the logistics of running their practice, preparing for meetings, and problem resolution. I support our clients in their journey as their point-person and concierge. My favorite comment to a client is: "I'll take care of it for you." And the support I receive in return is the best reward. I have a job that allows for motherhood, encourages independent thinking, and most importantly, plays a role in improving the lives of every single client that we welcome into our practice.

Sheila Evans
Practice Coordinator
Mosaic Financial Associates

FOREWORD

Many of our clients are doctors, some of whom are business owners, accumulating both business and personal assets. When clients accumulate wealth, they need to prioritize how to grow them and keep them protected.

The following pages will expand on the concepts and ideas I'm sure you have already considered if you are reading this. This book will provide the foundation and reference needed to embark on a challenging and extremely rewarding way of life.

Optimal Financial Health covers not only the basics for those doctors just getting started in practice, it also delves into enough details to perhaps "scare" some people into the action of prioritizing this very important element of a successful life. So many people understand the importance yet, quite simply, fail to adequately act on those understandings. Certainly, doctors are no exception to this phenomenon.

The basic theme provided: save it and grow it—then protect, distribute, and enjoy your disciplined approach. Those are the key elements to a successful life.

Life often complicates how to go about saving, growing, protecting, distributing, and enjoying the fruits of your labor. This book provides a wonderful foundational instruction manual that will allow anyone willing to put the fundamentals into practice to succeed with money.

TJ Casey, CPA
Udall & Casey, PLC

I

Getting Started

1

Introduction

If you are like most doctors, your time is at a premium. You have spent the majority of your young adult life in school and in training. After eight to twelve years of learning your specialty, the time has come to enter the professional workforce and enjoy the fruits of your labor.

Your future income will provide great opportunity but also some significant challenges. In our experience, the time our clients have spent in their medical training often leaves them ill-equipped to deal with personal and professional financial situations. These challenges generally lead clients down the path of anxiety, agitation, and playing catch up; all too often those emotions cross over into their personal lives as well. Most of our clients have asked questions pertaining to these challenges such as:

1. Is my family protected from a personal and/or a professional lawsuit?
2. What happens if I can no longer earn an income?
3. How much money do I need to retire?
4. When should I start saving or investing?
5. What is the best way to develop a savings/investing plan?
6. What should I know about with regard to my employer benefits?
7. Whom should I look to for advice?
8. How can I think about these issues while shouldering massive student loan debt?
9. I rotated with an attending who says he will never retire. What can I do so that won't happen to me?
10. How much should I spend on a home?
11. How do I minimize my tax burden?
12. I've heard I should protect my income. What are the key issues to consider?

13. What investments are most appropriate for me at this stage of my career?
14. What are the most common mistakes doctors make?
15. What is the value in evaluating financial issues while in training?
16. I've heard I should pay my home off as quickly as possible. Is this accurate?
17. Do I need life insurance? If so, what type best fits for me?
18. What issues should I consider when evaluating employment contracts?
19. How do I evaluate the differences among different practice environments?
20. How can I avoid the financial challenges my parents and colleagues face?
21. What asset protection measures should I evaluate?

These are only a few of the questions we have been asked; there are far too many to list here. The purpose of this book is to provide general guidance as a resource for doctors as they seek financial independence.

The question then becomes, "Are you one of the lucky ones?" Yes! We feel you can become lucky with deliberate forward-thinking and planning. You can sleep well at night knowing that you have taken steps to protect yourself and your family if tragedy strikes. You will know you are on the path towards achieving your financial objectives.

Now, begin your journey towards Optimal Financial Health and being Lucky.

2

Why Now?

A. Over the past nineteen years of our professional practice along with research and consultation with many doctors, we came to one dramatic conclusion: many of our clients suffer from IDILS. Unfortunately, there is no pill for "I'll Do It Later Syndrome". Often, depending on the individuals' personal or professional status, we hear the following:

1. "I'm in training now; I'll start looking at these issues closer to the end of my training."
2. "I'm too busy finishing training and interviewing. I'll start evaluating these issues when I get into practice and have money."
3. "I just started practice and have too much going on now; once I become a partner will be a better time."
4. "I'm single; these issues are irrelevant to me until I get married."
5. "We just got married and are too busy; we can wait to address these issues until we have children."

B. If people wait until they are several years into practice to begin the planning process (especially after partnership is achieved) the following things will happen:

1. They will continue to put off planning.
2. They will constantly feel behind.
3. They will increase their standard of living to meet or exceed their income ceiling.
4. The likelihood of achieving their goals decreases.
5. They may not achieve peace of mind regarding their financial situation.

In fact, one of the primary reasons we began speaking at teaching hospitals throughout the western United States is because our clients continually expressed to us the following: "I wish I had looked into these issues earlier. If I had, I would now be much further ahead than I am and probably wouldn't have made so many mistakes." They would then ask us to speak at the institution where they completed training, as well as to their colleagues at their existing practices.

The bottom line, however, is that there is a treatment for IDILS: The earlier you begin the planning process; you improve your chances for achieving your financial goals and objectives.

3

What is Luck?

The definition we use is "when opportunity meets preparation." Personally, we do not believe in luck. You may ask then, "Why write a book about being one of the lucky ones?" The answer is to demonstrate that you and you alone control the luck factor using our definition. Through your determination, motivation, and planning you will be more likely to achieve your financial objectives, goals, and dreams.

A. Okay, if we have the definition of luck in place, let's break down the two components. First, what is the opportunity? How many people do you know who can expect to transition from $40,000 per year in income to $200,000 or more? With this type of income increase, your opportunity is your ability to lay the foundation of your financial plan prior to establishing or increasing your standard of living. When you take a proactive approach to your planning anticipating the income increase, your likelihood of success increases tremendously.

B. Next, what are the steps involved in the **preparation**? Here are the fourteen steps.

1. **Identify Your Goals and Objectives.**
   You have likely heard about the power of visualization. When it comes to goal setting, it is well proven that people who visualize and write specific goals for their futures are more likely to achieve their goals, and obtain higher wealth than those who do not.

2. **Review Your Budget.**
   While in training, most doctors work in a cash-in cash-out environment. When reviewing your budget you will find areas of

opportunity as a result of unnecessary spending. Additionally, this exercise prepares you to turn your budget upside down. In other words, determine what your goals are and what they will cost, and adjust your expenses or standard of living accordingly. "Pay yourself first" is an expression supporting this idea of allocating monies to your goals first and then towards your standard of living.

3. **Establish an Emergency Reserve.**
   Create a "rainy day" reserve. Set aside enough cash to get you through an unexpected period of illness or unemployment; three to six months' worth of living expenses is generally recommended. Because you may need to use these funds unexpectedly, you'll generally want to put the cash in a low-risk, liquid investment, such as a money-market mutual fund or cash equivalent.

4. **Determine Children's College Education Funding.**
   Spouses' differing perspectives can result in disagreement about planning for education costs. For example, Anthony and his wife Wendy come from very different backgrounds: she from an extremely affluent family, and he from a middle-class family. As such, when they discussed having children and funding their education, it took some time to come to an agreement. Wendy wanted to plan to pay for everything because that was her experience; whereas Anthony felt it was important for the child to pay for his or her own education as he had. The key is to thoroughly discuss it in advance to determine a plan and course of action.

5. **Determine Retirement Objectives.**
   (a) When do you want to retire?
   (b) What is your retirement vision?
   (c) Do you want to live on less, equal, or more income in retirement than you did pre-retirement?

6. **Consider Parents and Inter-Generational Planning.**
   (a) Have your parents planned effectively for their future?

(b) Will you be financially responsible for them? If you are thinking about marrying, or are currently married, this is especially critical to address.
(c) What strategies exist for addressing this? Do they have a formal distribution plan? What is their plan for chronic debilitation?

7. **Assess Risk Management Strategies.**
Strive to protect against financial loss in the event of a death, disability of the wage earner, theft, or accidental loss of real or personal property, unforeseen liabilities, etc. In other words, a thorough understanding of the appropriate types and amounts of insurance coverage is important.

8. **Assess Asset Protection Strategies.**
(a) The first step is doing everything you can to prevent the lawsuit. However, in today's society, lawsuits seem to be unavoidable. Therefore, in addition to maintaining appropriate levels of malpractice and liability coverage, you should investigate strategies to help protect your family from personal financial loss.
(b) Are you in a position to consider more advanced planning strategies, such as trusts, offshore accounts, family limited partnerships, etc.?

9. **Consider Housing Expenses.**
(a) How much should you spend on your home?
(b) What tax efficiencies should be considered?
(c) Will you be "house poor?"

10. **Become Educated.**
(a) Books: The top five percent of income earners in 2010 earned $159,619 or more. This top 5% pays 60% of the overall federal tax revenue for this country[1]. When reading books published for the masses, review the information critically, and seek advice customized to your situation. We have found that for our clients, the information from most books about finances may not necessarily apply to their situations. The reason for

this is our clients are part of the top 5% of income earners. As such, they have specialized needs such as tax-efficient wealth accumulation, asset protection/preservation, and future estate tax and distribution concerns.

(b) *Other Resources:* People seek advice from a variety of people. As with books, it is important to critically evaluate each person's level of expertise. If you were having major surgery, chances are you would have a variety of specialists involved. The key is each specialist contributing where their specific skill set lies.

(i) Financial Planner/Investment Adviser Representative—we will address this later in the book.

(ii) CPA—typically provides specific tax or tax planning advice.

(iii) Attorney—the area of focus could include Asset Protection, Contract Review, and Estate Planning.

(iv) Family Member—perhaps a member of your family has financial success (maybe not) and provides advice. Is it specific to you and your situation? Is it up to date?

(c) *The Virtual Puzzle:* Pictures and anecdotes often make information easier to understand. We prefer to integrate these illustrative means with calculations. Often, advisors simply run basic calculations. Although this is a good starting point, the problem with basic calculation is the resulting plan is linear, which is not representative of taxes, inflation, and investment returns. Your individual goals are like the many pieces of a puzzle; as your goals change, the various pieces change, and subsequently the overall picture, i.e. the plan will change.

11. Develop the Blueprint and Action Plan.

Once you have established your goals, it is time to develop the blueprint. This blueprint serves as the foundation upon which all planning is built; it illustrates how to achieve your desired outcome. There is a significant difference between a financial plan and real life planning. No life experience is straight-line. There are many obstacles and speed bumps along the way. As such, your plan must have commitment and flexibility. Think of the action plan as a to-do list. When items are accomplished we check them off. As changes occur, expected or not, we check those off later.

12. **Initiate the 20% Guideline.**
    First of all, we are not fond of general rules of thumb. However, through the years, one question surfaced time and time again from our clients: "Can you give me a general rule of thumb of how much I need to save?" Keeping in mind the uniqueness of each client's situation, we developed the 20% Guideline. This general guideline for saving is saving 20% of your net (after taxes and retirement plan) income. We establish a goal for our clients to carve out 20% for their plan (Pay Yourself First) before they increase their standard of living in an effort to help them achieve their goals on time. We will cover this in another chapter.

13. **Implement the plan.**
    Maintain flexibility within a baseline. Begin with monthly savings/investing towards your goals: basic savings, portfolio development, college education funding, retirement, intergenerational planning, etc. Additional income is then applied to new goals or opportunities.

14. **Monitor and Adjust the Plan.**
    Annual reviews facilitate communication about the changes in your goals, as well as family or work situations. In addition, it also presents an opportunity to determine whether adjustments to your financial plan or implemented strategies are appropriate.

4

Budgeting

As mentioned previously, budgeting is a critical foundational element of successful planning. This being said, we thought it wise to provide two examples of budgeting. One is certainly more complex than the other so it's up to you to determine which one you wish to utilize.

We will start out with the simpler of the two.

Monthly Budget Worksheet

Mortgage / Rent	$
Utilities / Cable	$
Phone	$
Food / Groceries	$
Entertainment	$
Auto Insurance / Repair / Gas	$
Auto Payment	$
Student Loans	$
Credit Card Payment	$
Travel	$
Clothing	$
Charity/Tithing	$
Miscellaneous	$
Total Monthly Expenses	$

Monthly Income	
Less Total Monthly Expenses	
Total Monthly Surplus	

The second illustration is a tad more detailed.

- First, review your credit/debit card statements for the past year. Make certain to include all expenses. This exercise will help eliminate the "sometimes things just come up" excuse while also identifying savings opportunities when you say, "I had no idea I spent this much on X."
- Secondly, think of your money as going into three buckets each month:

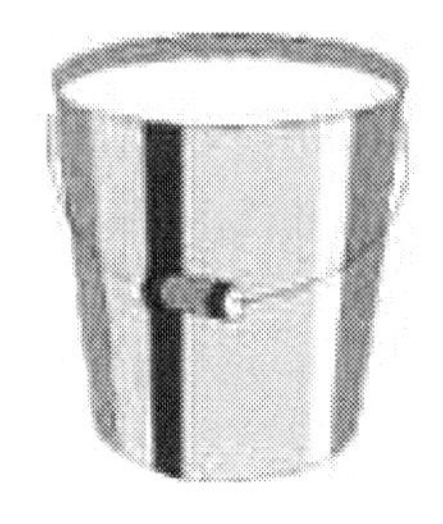

Bucket Number One:
Future Goals:
Savings, Investment

- **Retirement: $**
- **Emergency: $**
- **College: $**
- **Parents: $**
- **Other: $**

Bucket Number Two:
Monthly Expenses

- **Mortgage/Rent: $**
- **Energy/Utilities: $**
- **Loans/Cards: $**
- **Insurance: $**
- **Auto: $**
- **Other: $**

Bucket Number Three:
Monthly Surplus

- **A: Monthly Net Pay: $**
- **B: Savings & Fixed Expenses (Add Buckets One + Two): $**
- **C: Discretionary Money for Bucket Three (A-B): $**
- **Weekly Spending Allowance (C / 4.3): $**

- The key to this approach (as is true with savings/investing in general) is to automate everything.
- Set up two checking accounts: one from which to pay bills, the other for day-to-day expenses. The key is to pay yourself a salary

for the amount you commit to spending on a daily, weekly, etc. basis.

- This approach will help assure that you carve out a portion of income for goals, keep your expenses within the parameters of your goals, and also enjoy life.

5

Planning Considerations

What are the top planning considerations while in training? In our opinion, there are three planning strategies to evaluate while in training: one is investment-related; the other two are risk management-related.

- **Fund a Roth IRA.**
  You might say, "Why is it so important to fund a Roth IRA when I have such limited resources available to me?" The primary reasons are two-fold.
  - You might not be able to utilize a Roth once you complete training because you will make too much money. "Too much money?!" Yes, once your income exceeds certain levels (as of the printing of this book the income limits for a single household are $110k AGI and for married couples $173k AGI to fully contribute), it's quite possible the only years you are able to contribute to this vehicle is while in training.
  - The benefits of compound interest in a tax-free account are significant when considering long-term growth and future tax brackets. In subsequent chapters we discuss this in greater length. Suffice it to say, having money in a tax-free environment is very important.
  - As an example, if you were thirty years old and contributed $5k/yr (paid monthly) for a four year residency, at age 60, if the monies grew at 8%, you would have $186k tax free. If you waited to access the money until age 70, you would have $414,442. Recently at a presentation one of the attendees asked, "Am I totally hosing myself by spending the money I have on fun stuff rather than funding a Roth IRA?" My comment was, "You decide." We did the quick math

providing the outcomes. Now it's time for you to decide if you are "hosing" yourself.

- **Acquire Disability Insurance/Protect Your Income**.
  In our opinion, arguably the most important financial decision you will make upon deciding to become a doctor is to protect the investment you made in yourself. In other words, if you are unable to work as a doctor due to disability, you will continue to collect tax-free income from your disability policy. For your thorough review, Chapter 20 goes into greater detail about this vital matter.

- **Consider Life Insurance if You Have a Family**.
  Many of the people we've met through the years have asked a couple of questions regarding life insurance. The first question is, "If I don't have much money but I want to protect my family in the event I die what type of life insurance I should consider?" The second question is, "I've heard you should only by term or whole life insurance. What is your perspective?" The first question is relatively simple to answer in the sense that people are able to acquire relatively inexpensive term life insurance to protect their family. Further, you could purchase term insurance which affords you the ability to convert to permanent coverage in the future if appropriate for your situation.

  The second question is slightly more involved; however we'll answer it simply. When we hear the word "only" we become immediately focused on the agenda the representative has. In most cases, in our experience, when someone says, "only", as it relates to term or whole life, it's for two reasons. First, the company from whom they are paid pushes that product and/or idea. Secondly, the individual hasn't taken a comprehensive view of life insurance. If this individual did, they would realize there isn't one solution to this very important issue. In subsequent chapters we break this down in greater detail covering types and uses of life insurance. The bottom line is: if you want to protect your family in the event of your death, there are inexpensive ways to do it.

6

Does Debt Have You Down?

The key to evaluating debt payoff is a combination of your paradigm, or the lens through which you see debt, as well as, the hard numbers of the debt in question. In our experience people approach debt with two primary anchors: *financial sensibility* and *emotional sensitivity*. Financial sensibility involves evaluating two options, whereby if you had extra money in your budget on a monthly basis, would you financially be better off if you applied the money towards debt or to savings/investment. Emotional sensitivity involves your feelings about debt ranging from deep rooted discomfort, bordering on hatred, for debt no matter what the interest rate is, to total comfort.

Now before we go further, one of the first steps is to open your student loan envelopes (you might be amazed how many doctors in training do not do this). Regardless of how depressing it may be, these numbers represent your investment in yourself and you should be proud. Moving on, we will discuss three types of debt: credit cards, student loans, and home loans.

A. **Credit cards.**

In most cases, the emotional reaction to credit card debt is a different one than that toward other types of debt such as home or student loans. As a result of this strong emotional discomfort, we feel paying these off as quickly as possible is likely your best strategy. If you have credit card debt before establishing a savings/investment plan, we recommend paying the credit card debt out of the 20% rule set aside for savings. Once this credit card is gone, you are already in the habit of allocating the 20% and as such will have a fairly simple transition to savings/investing. This being said, if you are eligible for contribution to a Roth IRA, we should discuss potentially delaying payoff of this credit card as the long-term benefit of tax-free Roth IRA contributions may outweigh the short-term benefits of paying of the credit card. Running a side-by-side analysis of these two options is a useful exercise. Keep in mind, a majority of our clients will only be eligible to contribute to a Roth IRA while in training.

B. **Student loans.**

From the financial sensibility perspective, if you have low student loan interest rates, it would often make sense to let your great-great grandchildren pay off your student loans. Of course, this isn't a realistic option, but it is the thought behind the concept of financial leverage. Consider the following three student loan examples:

Student Loan Example #1

- *Loan Amount of $100,000*
- *Consolidated at 3% interest rate*
- *30 year payoff = $422 per month*
- *10 year payoff = $966 per month*
- *Difference in payments = $544 per month*

Option One: 30 year payoff plan, investing $544 difference each month.
Option Two: 10 year payoff plan, investing $0 for 10 years, then $966 for 20 years.

At the end of 30 years, here is the difference between Option one net worth minus Option Two net worth:

At 8% - $241,758
At 9% - $350,748
At 10% - $496,158

Student Loan Example #2

- *Loan Amount of $100,000*
- *Consolidated at 6% interest rate*
- *30 year payoff = $600 per month*
- *10 year payoff = $1,100 per month*
- *Difference in payments = $510 per month*

Option One: 30 year payoff plan, investing $510 difference each month.
Option Two: 10 year payoff plan, investing $0 for 10 years, then $1,100 for 20 years.

At the end of 30 years, here is the difference between Option one net worth minus Option Two net worth:

At 8% - $106,188
At 9% - $191,646
At 10% - $309,949

Student Loan Example #3

- *Loan Amount of $200,000*
- *Consolidated at 6% interest rate*
- *30 year payoff = $1,199 per month*
- *10 year payoff = $2,220 per month*
- *Difference in payments = $1,021 per month*

Option One: 30 year payoff plan, investing $1,021 difference each month.
Option Two: 10 year payoff plan, investing $0 for 10 years, then $2,220 for 20 years.

At the end of 30 years, here is the difference between Option one net worth minus Option Two net worth:

At 8% - $214,031
At 9% - $386,481
At 10% - $622,160

Result—Not only is the net worth higher with Scenario One with each set of parameters, but liquidity and budget flexibility are maintained. Imagine trying to go back to the student loan company after committing to the ten-year payment plan and asking to adjust the payment or asking for your money back! What would happen in the event of financial hardship if you had committed to the ten-year payment plan?

After presenting a similar example to one client having $250k of student loans at 5%, we received a much unexpected response: "One million dollars in thirty years does not mean more to me than $250,000 does today" (we illustrated the Option One payment plan from above at 10%). We immediately realized that the emotional sensitivity component of the paradigm far outweighed the financial sensibility component. We then asked the client a question: "What if, at the end of year five of your six year payback strategy [his proposal], you became financially debilitated? What if you could no longer earn an income? Could you go to your student loan carrier and ask for money back? Could you ask to have your payment lowered?" Here is the bottom line . . . if you were presented with a situation where your choice is to either default on your student loans or take care of your family, which would you choose?

Another consideration relating to student loans is to ensure that you obtain written copies of the promises made by any student loan consolidation counselor. Over the years we have seen too many instances where the presented arrangement is not honored and without a copy of these specifics in writing, our client has no recourse.

C. Mortgages.

First, let us say, there is no "right" way to manage this type of debt. But, the same principles covered earlier in relation to student loans may also apply exponentially to your home loan. As we mentioned previously, your financial situation is unique to the top 5% of income earners. So, from an income tax perspective, it may not make sense to pay your home off, as conventional wisdom might have you believe. Taxes are, or will be, the bane of your existence. Some of you, if still in training, will soon pay more in taxes than what you currently earn. Others among you already experience this tax burden. One of the primary ways to lower your tax liability is to take the interest deduction you gain from owning a home. The larger the mortgage you carry, the larger your potential tax deduction. Two words of caution: this is not an excuse to overextend or become "house poor." Second, be mindful of the maximum limits for a mortgage acquisition debt and home equity loans. Mortgage interest in excess of those limits is not eligible for an income tax deduction. It is crucial to review current tax laws pertaining to mortgage interest. It is also important to confer with an in-state advisor who can determine the extent to which your home is protected in the event of litigation. We will cover this in section II in more depth.

7

Entering Practice

This is arguably one of the most critical decisions you face as a doctor. Should I open my own practice, join a specialty group, join a large scale hospital/corporate practice, or go academic and become an attending?

Often the primary consideration in this decision is quality of life. Many of our clients have entrepreneurial aspirations and opening their own practice is highly desirable. For the past years they have worked tons of hours and have no challenge continuing that. Others might wish to join a hospital or academic institution, realizing that they may not make as much, but won't have to work as much either.

Income, time, and running a business are other considerations to evaluate. What amount of time do you want to spend on your practice? Do you want to have to handle the administrative aspects of the business, e.g. payroll, staffing, benefits, etc? These factors may lead you to open your own practice or join an existing practice.

Visiting with other doctors already established in their practice, along with professional advice will assist you in making the decision that is best for you.

If you should decide to operate your own practice or join a group where you are involved in day-to-day operations, please review the following check-list, brought to you by Ike Devji, J.D.

ESSENTIAL LEGAL AND FINANCIAL PLANNING CHECKLIST FOR BUSINESSES AND MEDICAL PRACTICES

The following is a basic "must have" checklist (in no order) that most of our business owner and doctor clients find to be indispensable. Many sources of loss or exposure can be easily planned for and addressed in a proactive manner.

The days of opening your doors and simply running a cash register are long gone; things are now much more complex. Keeping your wealth requires an experienced and sophisticated team and in some cases almost as much effort as making it in the first place.

Who's on your team? Do they have the skills and professional partners required to do the job or have you and your business outgrown them?

We see recurring patterns and common needs across many successful businesses. We help clients and their advisors all over the U.S. coordinate all or any of these issues with the team of professionals we have assembled to help maintain their hard earned success. Please review this list to see which areas you need to update or explore.

1. **Asset Protection Planning**—Think of it as **Net Worth Insurance**. Distancing you from your assets and protecting them from your personal and professional liability requires simple, cost effective and pro-active planning today while you still have well defined legal options. There is little or nothing to be done, except paying defense attorneys, if you get caught in a suit before you do something.
2. **Coordinated Financial Planning**—Making sure the money you make is working as hard for you as you worked for it and that the planning you have in place includes both growth and loss prevention strategies.
3. **Disability Insurance**—Protecting your cash flow against injury and illness, at the times you need it the most, is a critical step. Large amounts of coverage with lots of sophisticated bells and whistles are available. Also, make sure that your cross-purchase or buy-sell agreements are properly funded. If your partner has a stroke or some other debilitating illness, how long will you (or he) be willing and able to make large monthly payments to a non-productive partner?
4. **Liability Insurance**—Let's make sure it's enough, and then let's have a back-up plan (see item #1 above). This refers to both professional and personal liability coverage. These days we see multi-million dollar exposures from routine events like auto accidents on a regular basis.
5. **Life Insurance**—Make sure you have appropriate amounts to cover estate taxes, generate income for survivors and pay off debts you want settled. We also make sure that you are not paying too much and have

the most flexible policy with the greatest number of benefits. Again, cross-purchase and buy-sell agreements must be carefully funded. We routinely see these agreements between our business owner clients that are either unfunded or under-funded. If your partner dies with no coverage or inadequate coverage in place, you could easily find yourself across from their family in a courtroom explaining why the business should be liquidated to pay them the deceased's share.

6. **Workmen's Compensation Coverage**—Make sure that you and your employees are protected against injuries and their rising costs.
7. **Employee Benefits Planning**—From basic benefits like 401K to Executive Compensation planning, there are a number of ways to provide these benefits, some are more advantageous to you, the business owner, than others.
8. **Employee Handbook**—This document governs their rights and your responsibilities, controls actions in the workplace and establishes your employer policy. If you don't define certain policies, the courts (or worse . . . your employee's attorneys) will define them for you. This is one of the highest ROI (return on investment) investments you can make in your business in my opinion.
9. **Employee Dispute Resolution Package**—This prevents employee lawsuits and makes you a hard target, reducing your exposure. Right now employees win 75% of the time and the average sexual harassment verdict, as just one example, is at $530K. Your business is five times more likely to be sued by an employee than for any other reason. Have a plan.
10. **Proper Corporate Formation**—Is your formation or lack of it exposing you to liability and taxes? Will it hinder you in the case of sale? Do you have too many eggs in one basket? For example, if your practice owns the building it operates from, you are needlessly exposing the real estate asset to professional liability. Simple fixes can save you millions if something bad happens.
11. **Professional Accounting Service**—Do you have a good CPA? Taxes and payroll are just the beginning; have a professional at hand who proactively offers solutions and shows you legal tax avoidance options in addition to administrative and reporting functions we rely upon them for.
12. **Real Estate Depreciation / Property Tax Reduction Study**—Get tax deductions for depreciation now when you need them. You can

get large current deductions on your investment real estate in a safe and legal way.

13. **Income and Receivables Protection Planning**—Make sure the cash flow you use to fund all these other things is safe. Your income can be "equity-stripped" just like a piece of real estate and the value put within protected structures that grow them in a protected and tax advantaged way.
14. **Tax Reduction and Retirement Income Planning Including Pensions**—Remember this planning has to last at least 30 years and account for inflation! As an instant lesson, compare the cost of an automobile or a loaf of bread 20 years ago to their costs today and see if inflation made a difference. Imagine dealing with that kind of cost increase on a fixed income 20 years from today.
15. **Estate Planning**—Who gets what, when and at what cost in estate taxes? You can make the Estate Tax exposure number zero in many cases. We do not consider dying in 2010 (when the Estate Tax will be zero for a very short time) to be a good estate plan. Do you really think our current national debt will allow for doing away with this exposure? We and the tax and estate planners we work with don't.
16. **Exit Plan Strategy**—Ok you've been successful . . . now what? Make sure that your business is an asset when you want to leave and that the planning you have done minimizes your tax exposures on the sale or transfer. A little proactive work here can save you as much as 50% in taxes.
17. **Long Term Care Insurance**—The costs of this kind of care are soaring. Can you risk your retirement savings and family's legacy by not having it? Medicare has a five year look back and requires that you are nearly destitute before they cover essential daily care.

Additional Employment Considerations

Choosing the right career path is one of the most exciting and challenging decisions in a person's life. It is vital to take certain factors into consideration before you make this decision to ensure that you choose the path that is right for you. Consider the following:

- *Your Paradigm*: Your perspective on the interviewing process is a primary factor. For example, we counsel our clients to take the approach that they are interviewing the employer rather than the employer interviewing them. It is surprising how many people overlook the fundamental principle of protecting their interests.

- *Attorney Review:* It is very important to have an attorney review your employment contracts to determine the potential for conflicts or misunderstandings over provisions.
- *Fair Market Value*: Review the contracts to determine fair market value of the proposed income and be sure to compare multiple offers. The income amount should be compared to other groups in the same specialty and geographic area.
- *Perks*: Are there any sign-on bonuses or moving allowances? Are they comparable to other groups in the area? If offered, ask to have these funds released to you as soon as possible.
- *Speak to a Partner.* Invite the person who was just made partner out for coffee or lunch. Find out if they experienced any surprises or if, in hindsight, they have any questions they wish they had asked. Ask them if they like the other people with whom they work. An inside perspective is valuable in helping you to weigh your decision.
- *Non-Compete Clause:* Examine how the clause is structured and understand when it applies. Become aware of any possible financial repercussions you should expect if, in the future, your practice is found to be in violation of this clause.
- *Salary or Income Payment:* Identify and evaluate how your income is to be determined—by billing, collections, patients, etc.
- *Tail Coverage:* Determine the structure of your tail coverage. You should know whether or not you would have to pay for this coverage if you left the employer. If so, find out how that amount is determined. Additionally, identify how you would be protected in the event of a lawsuit against the group after your departure.
- *Nose Coverage:* Find out if this coverage is available and how it is structured.
- *Buy-in:* Determine the structure of buy-in. Ask questions pertaining to the amount, how it is paid (for example, is it a lump sum, part of a quarterly bonus, or some other structure)?
- *Partnership:* Questions to ask should include:

1. What is the time frame for prospective partnership?
2. How are partners paid?
3. Is there a separate formula used to determine individual pay?
4. After taking on expenses, will your pay go up or down?
5. Perhaps ask to review the Profit and Loss Statement if you are joining a smaller group without a public or proven track record of profitability.

There are a variety of questions to consider. The key is to get everything in writing! We are pleased to introduce Gary R. Blume, Attorney at Law, as a contributing author. He is an expert in contract review. He offers some important guidelines in the following section.

Physician's Guide to Commerce

EMPLOYMENT CONTRACTS

1. *Compensation*
   All employment arrangements with doctors should be with contracts with as much detail as possible. Fairness is the watchword. Be reasonable and not exploitive. Any person who feels taken advantage of is not going to be a good employee and partners who feel unfairly treated will not last in the long run. The employment situation can still be in place even if the doctor is a member of the corporation. Job duties, as well as termination procedures for a nonperformer and/or a person who does not fit need to be detailed. Compensation is the single largest issue with employees and partners. Discuss this carefully and thoughtfully. Additional items to be discussed are payment for malpractice insurance with tail coverage, payment for continuing medical education, paid benefits, vacation, retirement plans, expense reimbursement and health care coverage. Another issue with beginning doctors is whether or not bonuses or profit sharing arrangements are available. Look to what agreements are in place for senior doctors and with your peers. All you are seeking is equal treatment.

2. *Duties*
   Make sure duties under the contract are understood and spelled out. How many holidays are required to be worked? What is the nature of the service provided and what backups are in place? Again, the idea is fairness. Doctors do not want to always be assigned holidays and weekends while senior partners are always on vacation. As long as each doctor is treated in the same way and all are rotating, no problem will arise. Each doctor should be compensated for what they do.

3. *Covenants not to compete*
   Covenants not to compete are disfavored and the power of the clauses has been eroded in the last ten years. While a contract is still a contract, and the terms binding, many court created doctrines have been put in place to weaken the power of the clause. While this doctrine has been eroded, the idea of confidential information, trade secrets and patient lists has been given more protection. The doctor-patient relationship is a specific one and separate rulings have been provided to indicate it will be preserved. Doctors are also in a separate category of non—compete and confidentiality, as are attorneys, and are examined in a different light. For example, if a group of doctors has established a practice and a patient base and one of the physicians determines to leave, the new practice set up by the physician will be examined in terms of proximity to the existing practice, method of solicitation of patients, communications with existing patients by the current and new practice, and the overall impact on the departed practice. Care must be exercised to prevent disputes. Litigation over non-competes and confidential information is lengthy and costly. The analysis is specific to each situation and the standards are subjective and ever changing. Disputes are to be avoided.

CORPORATIONS

1. *Form a Corporation*
   All business operations should function under the protection of some form of limited liability entity. A corporation is a separate legal entity, in effect as an artificial person capable of entering into

contract, filing suit, being sued, purchasing assets, selling assets and acting through its officers, members, and agents. The corporation can conduct any lawful business. Licenses and permits will also have to be obtained for professionals in the field of medicine. It is important to keep the operation of the business separate from your personal assets. Multiple corporations can also be formed for each purpose. You can purchase a building to rent to the practice group, purchase vehicles to provide to the members, acquire and lease equipment to the practice, all utilizing separate entities for each express purpose. Each corporation can have a different form, can have different rights and interests of the participants and in the event of failure of one of the entities still allow the other entities under control of the participants to continue. This allows risk to be apportioned so a medical practice is not dependent upon the risks associated with real estate ownership and management, as an example.

2. *Select LLC, LLP, Professional LLC or Professional LLP*
   The Limited Liability Corporation (LLC) statutes in many states offer the most protection and flexibility as to form of entity. An LLC is a hybrid that combines tax advantages with express limited liability to its members. An LLC is owned by its members. The members can be in different classes, such as management members and profit sharing members. Since most medical businesses operate as a form of partnership, the LLC concept is a better fit than the structural INC forms. A large distinction with a general partnership is the liability of partners for the actions of the other partners. In the case of a limited liability member, none of the partners are personally liable for the conduct of the other partners. The corporation is liable for obligations of the corporation and the individuals are not. A rogue partner may abscond assets that could cause the demise of the corporation, but at least the liability stops there. The Arizona statutes recognize corporate, partnership, professional partnership and professional corporate forms. These have differences in management, financing, and control, but retain the essential protections of a corporation.

3. *Tax Analysis*
   A limited liability corporation can be treated as a sole proprietorship, partnership, C corporation or a sub S corporation at your election. This will allow you to select the form that is most advantageous to your particular situation taking into account your personal assets and other income.

4. *Familiarity with Laws*
   You must have a minimal level of understanding of the laws that will apply to you from a corporate and business point of view. It goes without saying that you must be familiar with insurance and medical rules and standards in your practice. Just because you are not an attorney or accountant does not mean that you should not be versed in the general laws and accounting procedures that apply to you. It is not always cost effective to pay an attorney or accountant to educate you on some matter that you can Google and learn in a matter of minutes. What is important is to understand when professional help is needed. The most important understanding you must have is of basic accounting. You will need to understand aspects of taxation, capital gains treatment, compensation in the form of dividends, salary or expense reimbursement, what qualifies as an expense, and how loans are accounted for. You will also need to understand how profitability is determined and how the capital accounts work. The subtleties of these items are for the experts, but you must have an overview so you can be conversant on what actions may or may not benefit you. You will also be required to be very familiar with medical rules on ethics, conflicts of interest, relations of outside businesses, kickbacks and allowed forms of compensation. You must also have a basic understanding of confidentiality agreements and any form of covenant not to compete. These are particularly difficult in the doctor situation where ethic overlays are in place.

5. *Personal Liability*
   In Arizona it is difficult to pierce the corporate veil and two requirements must be met: the corporation operates as the alter ego of the owners and the recognition of the corporate form would sanction a fraud or promote injustice. The alter ego concept is

one where the interests of the corporation and the owners have merged. Some factors are considered: undercapitalization, failure to maintain separate corporate documents, division of corporate property for personal use, lack of formalities in corporate meetings, and failure to maintain books and records of account in reasonable order. The courts have generally required the conduct of the persons to be separately actionable fraud to meet the second prong (corporate form sanction fraud/promote injustice). The effect of a successful attack on the corporate form results in individual liability on the part of the owners of the corporation.

6. *Liability to partners*
   With the development of the limited liability corporation, issues involving the liabilities of partners have been simplified. With a general partnership, a partner could take out a loan, remove all the cash from the business and all remaining partners would be liable. While the risk of this situation still exists, at least the liability will rest with the corporation and not be transferred to the members of the limited liability corporation. The solution is a series of checks and balances on the actions of any one member and the wise selection of partners without financial difficulties or substance abuse problems.

OPERATING AGREEMENT

1. *Rights of members*
   The operating agreement provides guidelines on the operation of the corporation. Typical items in the agreement include meetings, how to add members, how profits will be split, how decisions regarding control of the corporation are made, and how to dissolve the corporation. It is important to note that if you do not have a specific operating agreement, the Arizona Statutes will apply and provide necessary rules for the governance of the LLC. It is extremely important to have a custom operating agreement so all issues on capitalization, control, and membership entry and exit can be detailed. The statutes offer a simplistic approach to the management and could result in some very unfavorable treatment

of the members, or worse yet—allow a manager to retain control of the operations.

2. *Control*

   One of the most important issues is determining who controls the corporation. As discussed above, without an operating agreement to detail how control issues will be handled, the statutes will provide all answers. The operating agreement can be written to provide for an appointed manager (who may or may not own an interest in the corporation), a board of managers, or the members may manage the corporation with some majority vote arrangement, such as simple majority or a super majority: 75% of the members. Control of the operation can be divided into who makes decisions regarding medicine, finance, daily operations, and voting on dissolving the corporation. As long as the operating agreement is consistent with the wishes of the members, you will not be subject to any unknowns. The members could also appoint a committee that directs the activities of a specific manager, and the manager could operate under a budget or limitation on the manager's spending ability. Another formula involves creating different classes of membership interests with the Class A members, for example, exercising control and making decisions involving the direction of the company, and Class B members who share in the profits based on some predetermined formula. Persons could be both Class A and Class B members. The control issue, in the case of multiple classes of membership, is coupled with the compensation issue because the determination of the profit of a corporation could be with the Class A members, who may elect to incur additional expenses and salary to themselves so no profit gets to the Class B members. The Class B members have no say in what the profit will be, only an interest in sharing once the amount has been determined by the Class A members.

3. *Profit Sharing*

   The most difficult issue here is defining what the profit is. Can the manager decide to purchase Cardinals tickets? What if the management committee determines that meetings should be in Las Vegas? These are examples that, if they were not incurred, would make more money available for the partners in the form of profit or dividend payments. One solution is to provide a budget and specific expenses that will or will not be allowed. Just because the corporation shows a profit for the year does not mean money is in the bank and can be distributed. At the end of any year, the accountant will provide the calculated profit or loss of the business, and that profit or loss will be apportioned as determined by the members. This is different from a sub S corporation, which must distribute profits and losses according to the percentage interest of the shareholders.

4. *Meetings*
   Meetings are to be held, notes taken, and resolutions recorded. This relates to the issue of piercing the corporate veil. Corporations should follow corporate formalities to avoid seeming to be the alter ego of the principals. This includes having meetings to discuss actions and direction of the corporation. Large contracts, employment decisions and other financial matters should be determined by corporate meetings and resolutions.

5. *Financing Company*
   Financing is a critical issue facing any corporation. Funding sources are infinite in variety and can either be internal or external. A clear understanding of this has to be set out from the inception of the corporation. Where does the money come from to start the venture and where does money come from when the venture needs cash from time-to-time? Money provided to the corporation can either be paid-in capital or a loan. Each has advantages and disadvantages. If it is a loan, the funder will be paid back, but the corporation will be burdened with a loan payment. If contribution is paid in capital, the corporation does not have to pay it back and the funder will only receive the benefit when the corporation is sold in the form of a reduction in the capital gains to be paid because of the funder's basis in the corporation.

BUY/SELL AGREEMENT

The buy/sell agreement is a document in addition to the operating agreement that discusses the rights among the members of the limited liability corporation or among the shareholders of a corporation. Items contained in the buy/sell include the ability to use membership interest in the company as collateral, whether the interest can be sold or transferred, whether the interest is subject to a tag along right, drag along right, put or call option, and what will happen if the interest holder just wants out.

1. *Transfer of Interests*
   Usually, the interest is very personal to the person holding it. Due to the unique nature of professional services, patients cannot be readily transferred to another doctor, and the contribution of the doctor to the corporation is specific to that doctor.

2. *How to add members*
   The usual restriction is that all of the members must agree to add any additional member. Additional requirements can be in place: must be licensed physician, must contribute capital, can be a profit sharing member, must work full time for the corporation, etc. The new member can make payments to existing members (purchase a portion of their interest) or can acquire the interest by contributing capital. Each requirement will have certain tax considerations to examine.

3. *How to get out*
   The reason the member wants out or is forced out is important. If the member just wants out, a premium should not be paid to that member. Provisions can be in the buy/sell agreement to govern the valuation of the interest and how that value will be paid to the withdrawing member. Usual buy/sell agreements classify the reason as voluntary or involuntary. Just because a member wants out is a voluntary situation, whereas if the member has died or committed some crime, the situation is involuntary. Consideration should also be given to the situation where all or the majority of the members want to remove another member. This can benefit you if you are one of the members remaining, but can cut against

you if you are the member to be removed. I feel a provision should be in place that if the members do not like or do not want a certain member, that member can be removed. In general, within six months, the parties to an agreement can determine if they will play well together. Why not recognize this in the buy/sell and provide provisions for removal or reconstructing?

4. *Loans*
   Loans are in two varieties: to the members and from third parties to the corporation. All loans need to be discussed, and limitations put in place in great detail of what will and will not be allowed by the members. Usually the indebtedness to third parties of the corporation will have to be guaranteed by the members. Try to avoid this at all costs. The purpose of the corporation is to prevent liabilities from being transferred to the members. Financing the corporation with debt is good if the debt is used to acquire assets that will make money. If the debt is merely to pay bills to continue the business, it is not good. This is the debt spiral that is difficult to break.

5. *Sale of the company*
   Sale of the company must also be addressed. What if all the members except one want to sell the company? The drag along rights previously mentioned can solve the problem. As an example, in the buy/sell agreement, a clause could provide that if a majority of the members want to sell, they can drag along the remaining members, whether or not they want to sell.

6. *Sale of part of company*
   If the corporation is approached by a third party and seeks to purchase 40% of the corporation, should all the members be allowed to participate in the sale? This is the drag along situation. The buy/sell could have a provision that all members are entitled to participate on a pro rata basis in the sale. This prevents some of the members from cashing out and leaving the other members without any payment or participation. This, like the drag along right, can cut either way.

7. *Decision Making*
   Decision making encompasses all aspects of the operation of the practice. Who decides whether money should be borrowed, what employees to hire, what office equipment is needed, whether to fire someone, what benefits to offer, and on and on? The buy/sell is designed to cover decisions regarding the membership interests, but can also take into account the roles of the members. Perhaps a member will handle human resource issues and another deal with insurance. Many times when the business is starting, funds are not available to hire specific professionals to do these tasks. The buy/sell can make it clear that a particular person is responsible for a particular function and this is part of the consideration for the membership interest. If this is the case, I suggest that the person doing the function be paid for the work separately from their practice. This way, you do not go down the road of "I'm working harder than you" arguments.

8. *Capital Contributions*
   This must be spelled out in detail. Are all the members subject to capital calls? These details can also be in the operating agreement and make them corporate obligations of all members. In some situations, you may have groups of members: founders, junior partners, associates, etc. Each can have different compensation and profit sharing agreements. Junior members cannot feel burdened by the old members. This can be part of the plan of succession to keep the corporation functioning and to define what kind of exit strategy will be in place. This must be detailed or the business will fall apart. Young members need to feel they will be compensated fairly and in a similar manner as the founding members. The buyout of retiring partners must be discussed and understood by all members.

9. *Buyouts*
   The buyout arrangement can be whatever is decided but it should not provide for 'no payment' to the departing physician. In some practices, the old doctors try to sell the corporation they own or take it public and receive the lion's share of the benefits and cash. This will harbor resentment in those not participating and will

guarantee the deal will not go through. The first examination involves the question: what is the purpose of the corporation? It might be to have a group of doctors merely hiring employees and managing the practice to exploit the young employees as much as possible. If you expect doctors to provide their best efforts and to contribute to the corporation as a whole, you will have to plan for a way they can receive the same benefit all senior doctors receive. This may involve a stepped approach to retirement and compensation. The longer you are present, the more you will receive in retirement credits and compensation. Be careful how this is structured; it is the cause of much rancor.

BUSINESS VENTURES

Remember that you are an expert in a limited field: medicine. This does not give you insight into real estate, technology or any other business venture. When you get involved with a non familiar business venture, provide for two things: hire someone you can trust who is an expert, and only invest the amount (including long-term risk capital) that you can afford to lose.

1. *Form of Venture*
   Business associates range in structure from unincorporated associations to joint ventures to fully reporting public companies. These situations tend to be unique and are specialized according to the intent of the participants. As an example, a group of like service providers could make the decision to become a public company and issue stock to persons in exchange for the doctors being employees of the corporation. Business ventures can be formed outside the function of providing medical services to patients. An example is owning and operating an MRI business to provide a specialized service to many clinics and doctors. Additional ventures are formed by physician groups in unfamiliar businesses. From 2005 to 2007, many physicians got involved in real estate speculation. You know how that turned out.

2. *Control*
   The venture can be managed by a manager or the members. The more members, the more difficult it is to manage. Voting and approval of actions is difficult. The manager can also be a committee of members for ease of operation. A manager does not have to be a member and can be a professional selected to run the operations including insurance, benefits, employment issues, contracts with vendors, and office work flow.

3. *Risk*
   All business is the assessment and apportionment of risk. Determine the scope of the venture and who the potential predators are. Vendors, landlords, patients, competitors, and regulators are all potential predators and each must be examined. Separate all risks that can be insured and obtain an appropriate amount of insurance to cover the worst case situation. Malpractice is the largest risk and must be diligently assessed and dealt with. In ventures that are not medical, insurance is still your strongest line of defense. You can get errors and omissions of interest for the directors and officers, general business insurance, and specific packages depending on the type of venture.

4. *Capital*
   Risk only what you are willing to lose. Protect your core practice as much as you can. If the venture folds, you can always earn a living with the practice. Too many physicians risk too much, causing difficulty in the underlying practice.

II

Grow Your Wealth

8

The 20% Guideline

What it is

This guideline is the foundation of becoming Financially Healthy or taking advantage of the opportunity available to you. In our practice, a majority of our doctors in training complete their program between the ages of 30-35. Thus, the 20% guideline provides the additional funding needed to bridge the gap to early retirement, pay for education funding and potential purchases, and provide a tax hedge, etc.

Why it is used?

This benchmark rule is a guideline used to establish how much to save. Visiting with an advisor will be necessary to determine which level of savings is appropriate for you and where these dollars will be allocated, as it will be different for each person based on their goals.

When to use it

The time to implement this strategy is immediately upon completion of training. For example, let's say you earn $50,000 while in training and your practice income is $250,000. If you contributed modestly to a retirement plan at $20k, and saved 20%, how difficult would it be to live on $170,000 (taxes and retirement contribution considered)? In over ten years, we have never had a client or their spouse suggest that living on $170,000 per year will be a challenge.

The following chart shows the projected earnings of a $50,000 yearly investment (contributed monthly) over 20 years at 6%, 8%, and 10%.

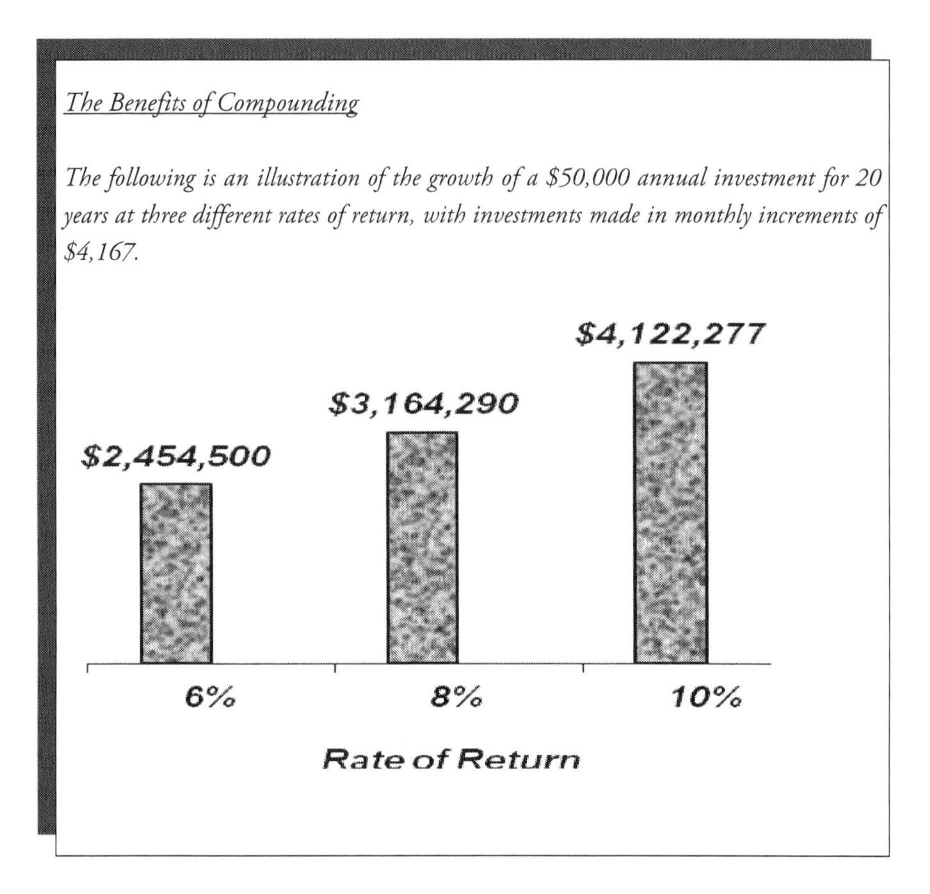

The Benefits of Compounding

The following is an illustration of the growth of a $50,000 annual investment for 20 years at three different rates of return, with investments made in monthly increments of $4,167.

On the other hand, consider a client who has already been making $250,000 for some time. How likely is it that this client would carve out the 20% for savings, investing, or anything else? In fact, we have a client earning $500,000 annually who struggles to save $1,500 per month-$18,000 per year. In a recent meeting, this client expressed frustration because he likely wouldn't hit his financial goals. We explained to him that he could reach his goals if he was willing to adjust his standard of living. As you can imagine, this was not a comfortable discussion for him and his wife, nor will it be an easy transition of their income allocation.

To further illustrate the power of starting to save early in your career:

The Cost of Waiting to Begin Investing

Here is the monthly investment required to accumulate $1,000,000 by age 65, assuming an average 10% compounded rate of return.

Age to Begin Investing	*25*	*35*	*45*	*55*
Monthly investment Amount to reach $1,000,000 Goal	*$158*	*$442*	*$1,316*	*$4,882*

The Objective of the 20 % Guideline

The objective is to position yourself to take advantage of the opportunity of a sizeable income increase upon entering practice and ultimately to achieve your financial objectives. The key is to carve out some number, some percentage of your new income immediately prior to adjusting your standard of living. Now go make yourself lucky and of Optimal Financial Health!

9

A New Way to Look at Debt

Financially, paying off your mortgage may not be in your best interest for many reasons. It is important for each individual to evaluate their specific situation taking into consideration their goals, income, available interest rates, etc.

Emotionally, your sensitivity towards debt is a strong component. But, consider what would happen if your income was lost through disability, or some other unforeseen crisis? Should financial debilitation occur; assets such as a mortgage-free home may be at risk if liquidity is needed for current expenses. At the same time, it may also be difficult to continue making mortgage payments without income. Depending on the state in which you live, state laws regarding mortgage debt may or may not assist your family in the event of judgments and/or foreclosures. Proper leveraging of mortgage debt should be carefully considered and reviewed when purchasing a home.

Another potential strategy, which uses the financial sensibility component previously discussed, is to make the smallest possible down payment. The following example shows how two differing down payment scenarios affect wealth in various circumstances. When considering the example below, determine what is appropriate for your situation:

Home Mortgage Illustration

- Home Purchase Price: $100,000
- Person A: debt averse and pays cash
- Person B: put 5% down, and invests $94,000
  - takes out a $95,000 interest only mortgage
  - pays $1,000 of mortgage acquisition costs

- Each person has $100,000 of capital available and has annual cash flow of $7,000 available
- Each person is in a 30% income tax bracket
- Housing values in the area appreciate 5% annually
- These are the only factors included in this analysis

Result After One Year	*Person A*	*Person B*
Home Value	*$105,000*	*$105,000*
Mortgage owed	*$0*	*$95,000*
Equity in Home	*$105,000*	*$10,000*
Invest capital at 8%	*$0*	*$101,520*
Invest cash flow at 8%	*$7,650*	*$0*
Invest income tax savings from mortgage interest at 8%	*$0*	*$2,100*
Results after one year	*$112,560*	*$113,000*

Result After Five Years	*Person A*	*Person B*
Home Value	*$127,628*	*$127,628*
Mortgage owed	*$0*	*$95,000*
Equity in Home	*$127,628*	*$32,628*
Invest capital at 8%	*$0*	*$138,117*
Invest cash flow at 8%	*$44,351*	*$0*
Invest income tax savings from mortgage interest at 8%	*$0*	*$13,305*
Results after five years	*$171,979*	*$184,050*

Under this simplistic example, where the interest expense on the mortgage debt is less than the investment earnings on invested capital, Person B comes out ahead. But, keep in mind that Person B has taken on more risk. If investment earnings fall, any advantage to Person B would be eliminated. It is crucial for a home owner to thoroughly understand these risk/return issues and how their cash flow may be affected by a career interruption or long-term disability. You are advised to consult your tax professional when making these decisions.

The average person retires on 70% to 80% of their pre-retirement income, as a result, most of them will enter retirement in a similar tax bracket as they experienced before retirement. Taking cash from investments to pay off the mortgage balance eliminates one of the last remaining tax breaks. This might not be in a high income earners best interest. Also, there are other factors to consider. Children no longer live at home, no further 401k contributions are being made, and you will likely have no business deductions, taking away the most commonly used tax-lowering strategies. Additionally, you must consider that your exposure to litigation does not diminish upon retirement. Having a huge chunk of equity in your home might expose you to potential legal threats depending on the state in which you live.

Your income and your potential for lawsuit are greater; therefore your strategy should be different. It is important to base your strategies on your unique facts and situation which is likely different from a majority of income earners.

Another variable to consider with home debt is the sensibility in paying off the loan at an accelerated rate. For example, what if your desire was to pay off the home loan in 15 years as opposed to thirty? Again, there isn't anything wrong with this strategy; however we encourage clients to look at this decision from a different perspective. What if you were still able to pay off your home from out of pocket money in 15 years, while also growing your wealth, maximizing your tax deduction, and lessening the impact of would-be creditors? The following table illustrates the strategy of selecting a thirty year loan but taking the difference of fifteen and thirty year payments to an equity indexed universal life insurance policy (EIUL).

	Homeowner A	Homeowner B
Mortgage	$1,000,000	$1,000,000
Term	30 Years	15 Years
Interest rate	6%	5.5%
Principal and Interest Payment	$5996 / month	$8171 / month
Payment Difference →	$2175 per	month
Over-funded IUL policy	$2175 / month	$0
Death Benefit Provided from IUL Policy	$775,000	N/A
Total Monthly Outflow	$8171 / month	$8171 / month
Tax-free cash flow from IUL Policy Year 16 to 30	$5970 / month (pays to mortgage)	$0
Tax-free cash flow from IUL Policy Year 31 to Age 100	$5970 / month (enjoys for retirement)	$0

Another way to evaluate the financial sensibility of paying down your home more quickly is to consider the following. What if you were considering the decision of paying extra on a monthly basis to your home in an effort to pay it off sooner? The following table illustrates the outcome to your wealth over a thirty year time frame by taking that extra money and placing it in a side-fund, rather than the home. The parameters of this example are a male age 35 (super preferred—best rating classification), with a variable loan rate of 6.5%.

	Homeowner A	Homeowner B
Mortgage	$400,000	$400,000
Term	30 Years	15 Years
Interest rate	5.5%	5%
Principal and Interest Payment	$2271 / month	$3163 / month
Payment Difference	→ $892 per	Month
Over-funded IUL policy	$892 / month	$0
Death Benefit Provided from IUL Policy	$325,000	N/A
Total Monthly Outflow	$3163 / month	$3163 / month
Tax-free cash flow from IUL Policy Year 16 to 30	$2425 / month (pays to mortgage)	$0
Tax-free cash flow from IUL Policy Year 31 to Age 100	$2425 / month (enjoys for retirement)	$0

As these tables illustrate, the same end goal of early home payoff can be accomplished with vastly different results. Homeowner A not only enjoys an improved net worth, they also are in a position of additional flexibility should cash flow change. (See Chapter 21 regarding specifics of IUL—Indexed Universal Life)

10

Investment Strategies and Suitability

Nostradamus said there are things we cannot predict. Two such impossible predictions are whether the market will rise or fall and which sector of the market will perform well one year to the next. There are two strategies that help to alleviate the guesswork.

A. Dollar Cost Averaging

This principle is based on the maxim, "Buy low and sell high." This strategy helps you successfully pursue the "buy low" portion of that maxim, by allowing you to buy shares of a security at a lower average cost than the average share price. The key to successful investing is a consistent, disciplined, automated approach.

For example, let's say you have $500 to invest over five months. One strategy is to place all the money into the investment immediately. Another strategy is to allocate the amount monthly. Over the five months, the share price goes from $10, $5, $2, $5, and $10. In the first strategy you would still have $500 at the end of five months. In the second strategy you would have $1100. The concept is to buy more shares when the price is low and buy fewer shares when the price is high. It's like shopping at Nordstrom's half-yearly sale; you can buy quality goods at a lower price.

For further illustration, consider the following example.

Dollar Cost Averaging

Month Purchased	*Investment Amount*	*Share Price*	*Shares Purchased*
January	$1,000	$40	25
February	$1,000	$50	20
March	$1,000	$40	25
April	$1,000	$25	40
May	$1,000	$40	25
June	$1,000	$50	20
Totals	$6,000		155

Average Share Price: $40.83
Average Cost Per Share: $38.70
Difference / Savings Per Share: $2.13

1. **Take emotions into account.** Often when people invest, fear and greed are their primary emotions. With the Dollar Cost Averaging approach you worry less about ebbs and flows of the market or when to buy or sell because you are investing on a systematic basis. You are as likely to invest when prices are low as when they are high.

2. **Market timing does not work.** Peter Lynch of Fidelity Investments and investor and CEO Warren Buffet have both spoken out against market timing, saying that success comes from time in the market rather than timing the market.

As you can see by the graph below*, missing out on the best 30 months over an eighty year time frame dramatically impacts your growth.

Market Timing: An Expensive Strategy

The 2010 value of $1.00 invested in 1926:

- *Large Company Common Stocks* *$2,361.58*
- *Large Company Common Stocks Minus the 30 Best Months* *$33.52*

**Source: "Large Company Stocks—Standard & Poor's 500". Calculated and presented using Ibbotson Investment Analysis Software.*

B. Asset Allocation

We do not have a crystal ball indicating which sector in the market will do well from one year to the next. With a consistently rebalanced portfolio, again we can lessen the emotional aspect of investing while maintaining the portfolio in line with your personal risk/tolerance profile. Another component beyond traditional asset allocation (based on Modern Portfolio Theory—don't put all your eggs in one basket) is utilizing alternative asset classes, such as Managed Futures, Commodities, and Publicly non-traded REIT's (Real Estate Investment Trusts).

Risk Reduction Illustration

Example using date of October 19, 1987

Portfolio #1	100% Stocks
$10,000	Investment
- 2,300	Single Day Loss
$7,700	**Remainder**
Portfolio #2	50% Stocks / 50% Bonds
$10,000	Investment
- 1,150	Single Day Stock Loss
$8,850	
+ 600	Single Day Bond Gain
$9,450	**Remainder**

While this top-ten list shows a rocky ride, as the above table shows, the single largest percentage daily loss on October 19, 1987 was 22.6% which at the time was only 508 points.

Top 10 Single Biggest Daily Point Losses of the DOW

Date	***Points***	**%**
08/04/2011	513	6.4
10/22/2008	514	5.7
10/27/1997	554	7.2
4/14/2000	618	5.7
8/8/2011	634	5.5
10/9/2008	679	7.3
12/1/2008	680	7.7
9/17/2001	685	7.1
10/15/2008	733	7.9
09/29/2008	778	7.0

Consider this example which shows how investors can mitigate some of the risk of market loss while potentially growing their wealth by diversifying via asset allocation.

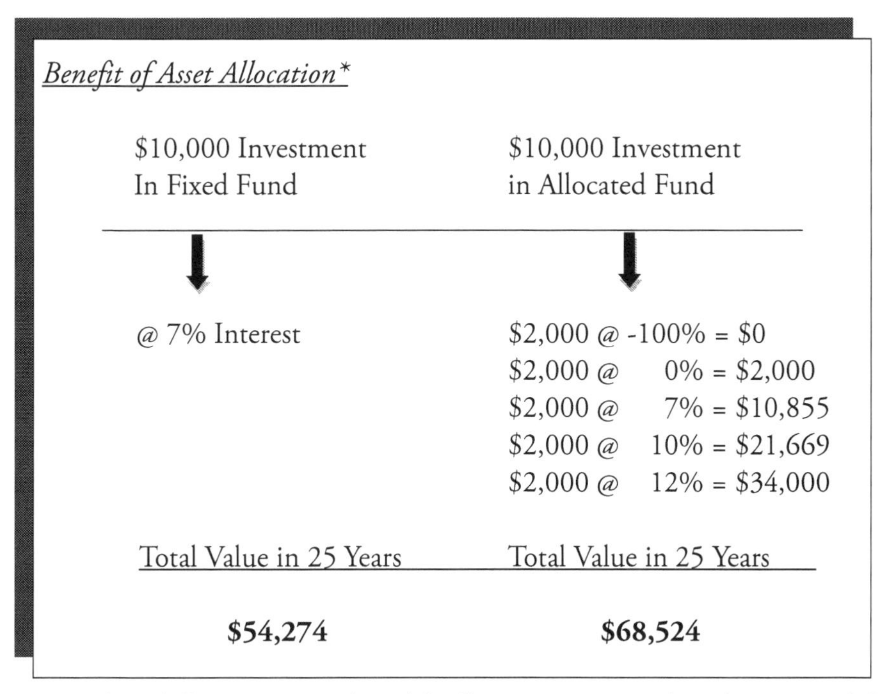

**Hypothetical Illustration: Hypothetical for illustrative purposes only and is not intended to represent the past or future performance of any specific investment. Rates of return will vary over time, especially for long term investments. Actual results will wary. Investments offering the potential for higher rates of return also involve a higher degree of risk.*

There are two other variables to consider in the realm of investment strategy and suitability. First, what is the opportunity cost on your investment, and second, what criteria are utilized to determine investment suitability?

A. *Opportunity Cost*

One of the many challenges our clients face is that as their non-tax deferred investment portfolio grows, their tax liability increases. Often we are asked the following questions relating to the investment portfolio:

(a) What is this 1099 DIV tax form we received? Or, if applicable, why did I receive one even in a down market?
(b) Why am I paying extra taxes?
(c) When will I ever use this money?

The real question should be, "What is the opportunity cost on the monies used to pay the tax?" In other words, what would the tax monies have grown too, if instead of paying taxes via the gains on this medium term portfolio had the monies stayed invested in a tax efficient environment? With capital gains tax rates at historical lows since 2001, we've become accepting of the qualified dividend and long-term capital gains tax rates available. As we are all aware, capital gains tax rates are set to increase in 2013. Additionally, with our current economic state of affairs, the potential (likelihood) for this to remain the case or increase is something to strongly consider. Will your non-tax-deferred investments be crippled by this reality? If so, what is your plan?

B. *Criteria of Investment Suitability*

The following are three criteria we often use to determine the appropriate vehicles for our clients to achieve their goals. In the next chapter we will discuss tax considerations as additional criteria.

1. **Accessibility/Time Frame**. When deciding on which type of investment vehicle to pursue, it is important to determine how long you can afford to tie up the invested dollars. Remember that short-term investments are generally not appropriate for long-term objectives and vice versa. For example, a variable annuity, 401k, or individual stocks probably aren't appropriate for accomplishing short-term goals any more than a money market would be for a thirty-year investment time frame.
2. **Risk/Volatility**. There are questionnaires and other tools available to aid in determining individual risk tolerance. Risk tolerance refers to how comfortable you are with market volatility. Can you tolerate watching your investment accounts go up and down with the market, but giving you an opportunity for higher returns? Or, are you more comfortable earning a fixed rate of return even if it is lower? It is important to match your portfolio with your individual tolerance.
3. **Asset Protection**. Is the investment vehicle afforded statutory protection from potential judgments? Will you need to enhance your protection using other vehicles?

11

Tax Efficiency and Growing Your Wealth

One of the primary considerations when growing your wealth is tax efficiency. Often people focus only on the present, when they should also consider the potential tax efficiency over time and into their retirement years.

A. *Bucket Strategy*

Your investments fit into three categories, or buckets.

1. **Fully taxable** investments require you to pay taxes on investment income earned and capital gains recognized each year (savings accounts, stocks, certain types of bonds, CDs or mutual funds not in retirement accounts).
    (a) *Mutual fund features*: Dollars are contributed after-tax. During the growth of the investment, annual distributions by the mutual fund are periodically taxed. In addition, any time you rebalance your portfolio, any gains on the shares sold are taxed (we generally will want to follow an asset allocation strategy, as well as avoid taxes which creates a conflict). Finally, when you cash out or sell your mutual funds you will pay tax on any gains which have not yet been taxed.
    (b) *Stock investment features*: Again, you will have a tax liability when you rebalance your portfolio and by selling stock realizing a gain. For active traders who rarely hold a stock for longer than a year, this tax is at their ordinary income tax rate. For stocks (and mutual funds) held longer than 12 months, gains on shares sold will be taxed as long-term capital gains. Currently that rate is 15% for federal income

tax payers in the 15% ordinary income tax bracket or higher. These tax rates are set to expire at the end of 2012. At the time of publication, long-term capital gains tax rates are set to revert to the previous 20%.

2. **Deductible Tax-deferred** investment vehicles accumulate without recognition of tax liability. However, principal and gains are taxable upon withdrawal at ordinary income tax rates (whatever those might be at time of withdrawal). Make your own conclusions as to where you think tax brackets will be when you retire! Examples include qualified retirement plans such as traditional IRAs, 401ks, SEPs, TSAs, and pension plans.
   (a) Pre-tax/tax-deferred investments' features: These dollars are contributed on a pre-tax basis, allowing you to lower your income tax liability today. The invested money grows tax-deferred (no tax liability while funds remain in the account), with the dollars taxed upon withdrawal.
   (b) Restrictions: If you access the accounts prior to age 59 ½, you will pay a 10% early withdrawal penalty (although some exceptions to this penalty may apply). Additionally, at age 70 ½, you are required to take required minimum distributions (RMD) from the account each year using one of the three IRS approved methods of calculation. Failure to take those distributions beginning after age 70 ½ can result in additional significant tax penalties.

3. **Tax-advantaged** investments grow tax-free and can provide tax-advantaged income (municipal bonds, cash values of life insurance, 529 plans, and Roth IRAs).
   (a) After tax/tax-advantaged investments' features: Dollars are contributed after-tax. The dollars grow tax-deferred while in the account. Taxation upon accessing the money varies by investment type. For instance, non-qualified annuity distributions of growth and interest are subject to tax while the cost basis in the annuity is received free of tax. Withdrawals from Roth IRA's can be received tax-free if it meets the definition of a qualified distribution. Cash values of life insurance can be accessed on a tax-advantaged manner

through policy loans and withdrawals of basis. Please note that municipal bonds may be subject to the Alternative Minimum Tax (AMT).

Many of our clients come to us with too much in the fully taxable bucket, not enough in the tax-deferred bucket, and almost nothing in the tax-advantaged bucket. So the question we pose to you is, "Would you rather pay taxes on the seed or the harvest?"

B. *Understanding Tax Brackets*

The first step is to understand how tax brackets work. Often clients ask, "What tax bracket am I in?" Others make assumptions like the following: "I am in the 45% tax bracket," or "I jumped into the next tax bracket this year." We once had a client who considered taking a contract with less pay because they felt their net income from the higher paying job would actually be lower after taxes. This is simply not true. The concept to understand is that federal income taxes are calculated on a graduated scale; taxpayers will have the benefit of lower rates on a portion of their income. (Note: This may not be true if you become subject to the (AMT).

***2012 Federal Tax Brackets*[1]**

Tax Bracket	*Single*	*Married Filing Jointly*	*Head of Household*
10% Bracket	$0-$8,700	$0-$17,400	$0-$12,400
15% Bracket	$8,700-$35,350	$17,400-$70,700	$12,400-$47,350
25% Bracket	$35,350-$85,650	$70,700-$142,700	$47,350-$122,300
28% Bracket	$85,650-$178,650	$142,700-$217,450	$122,300-$198,050
33% Bracket	$178,650-$388,350	$217,450-$388,350	$198,050-$388,350
35% Bracket	$388,350+	$388,350+	$388,350+

As you can see by the tax table, a married household with an annual adjusted gross income of $400,000 (not subject to the AMT), the entire $400,000 is not exposed to the 35% rate, only the taxable income above $388,350. So, from a financial planning perspective, it is important to identify how much your last dollars earned are being taxed, since that is where the tax-savings will have the most impact. In this example, $11,650 in income would be taxed at the highest bracket, 35%.

Please see Appendix I titled "Understanding Tax Brackets" for more information.

C. *Controlling Your Money*

Our goal for our clients is for them to have control over their money no matter what happens to tax rates. We know tax laws, including tax rates and income brackets, change year to year. This is why it is so important to have exposure to a variety of investments with different tax treatment. Frankly, even if taxes were to remain the same over time, your unique financial situation: high incomes, with high tax brackets, and exposure to litigation, alone makes diversification important. You must also consider the tax ramifications you will face in the future. Members of the Baby Boomer generation tend to be poor savers. For example, of the 70 million living Baby Boomers, half are dependent on entitlement programs such as Social Security, Medicare, and Medicaid. By their sheer numbers, they have generated significant federal income tax revenue for this country. However, as they move into retirement, their standard of living is projected to be lower, thus, generating less tax revenue for the country. As people age, the likelihood of increased health care costs is almost certain. What does this have to do with taxes? Think of a business facing both declining revenues and increasing expenses. Do the math and only one conclusion comes to mind; increased costs and higher taxes. In subsequent chapters, we will cover this in greater depth.

D. *Tax Diversification Example*

Tax Diversification Example

Parameters

- *Both Clients' Income* = $200,000
- *Both Clients' Goal* = Go Part-time at Age 55, Retire at 60, Maintain standard of Living
- *Tax Rates*: $0 to $100,000 Annual Income = 25% Tax Rate
  $100,000 to $200,000 Annual Income = 50% Tax Rate
- **Client A** has 100% of their retirement assets in tax-deferred, **taxable** environment (ex. IRA, 401k, 403b, SEP IRA)
- **Client B** has 50% of their retirement assets in tax-deferred, taxable environment and 50% in tax-favored, **tax-free** investments (e.g. Roth IRA, cash value life insurance)

Results at Age 55	Client A	Client B
➢ Earned Income =	$100,000 @ 25% tax	$100,000 @ 25% tax
➢ Retirement plan=	$100,000 @ 50% tax	$100,000 tax-free
➢ Early W/D Penalty	$10,000	
Taxable Income =	$200,000	$100,000
Average Tax Liability= (+ Early W/D Penalty)	42.5%	12.5%

Results at Age 60	Client A	Client B
➢ Retirement Plan=	$100,000 @ 25% tax	$100,000 @ 25% tax
	$100,000 @ 50% tax	$100,000 @ tax-free
Average Tax Liability=	37.5%	12.5%

Conclusions

Client B maintains the flexibility to adjust retirement distribution strategies as tax environments change throughout retirement. Whereas Client A is limited to fully taxable distributions at all times.

Though this is a simplistic example, it illustrates that diversification of the tax treatment in the investment vehicle selected is critical to the planning process. Your financial plan will be subject to different tax brackets, more complex challenges and opportunities, as well as frequent changes. As a result, it is important to recognize the benefits of diversification, which you will reap both before and during retirement.

12

Debunking Three Common Tax Myths

Here are three of the most common presumptions about retirement that many people make, usually supported in general literature on the subject.

- **Myth #1: You will be in a lower tax bracket when you retire.** Conventional wisdom suggests it is always better to push taxes into the future because you are likely to be in a lower tax bracket, due to a reduction in income after retirement. Do you want lower income in retirement? We know better than to hope that the IRS will reduce the tax rates. Most of our clients will be in a similar or potentially higher tax bracket during retirement so we must plan accordingly.
- **Myth #2: You will not need as much money in retirement to maintain your current standard of living.** In over 19 years, we have never had a client suggest that they would like to have a reduced standard of living during retirement. Taking into consideration variables such as inflation, travel, and rising health care costs to name a few, it will likely cost more to maintain the same standard of living.
- **Myth #3: Your investments, assuming an average rate of return, would grow in a straight line.** The key here is to realize the market has historically experienced significant swings. *When* these swings occur it will greatly impact your retirement income. As such, tax efficient investing is critical to your success.

In this publication, we cannot begin to scratch the surface of the tax issues pertaining to qualified retirement distributions. According to a 2010 report by Employee Benefits Research Institute (EBRI), people over sixty employed for thirty or more years had about $200,000 in their 401k while people in their fifties are poised to retire with similar account balances. What is the balance in your 401k? What will yours be worth when you retire? Clients often tell us that everyone tells them to max out their 401k account. Or, they wonder why they haven't heard more about using other tax-advantaged investments. Our experience is, due to the uniqueness of our clients' situation, many magazine articles, books, and other publications which are often directed towards the masses may not apply to your situation. The bottom line is to make sure to diversify your tax exposure utilizing a variety of investment vehicles.

13

Scary Math: Where are taxes headed and What are you going to do about it?

Most people don't like to think about taxes, but smart people will take the time to ask themselves: am I prepared for the future? Have I evaluated tax brackets? Have I done the math? Have I prepared my distribution strategy accordingly? What will happen when I die?

Many people are mistaken when they assume they know which tax bracket they can expect when they reach age 60 and age 70. Do you think your tax bracket will be higher or lower than it is today? Consider the following data.

In order to understand where our tax dollars go, become familiar with the three categories of our federal budget:

1. Mandatory spending: federal funding that continues each year without Congress having to approve it. Social Security, Medicare, and Medicaid comprise almost 70 percent of all mandatory spending. Consider these facts.

    - Half of the 70 million Baby Boomers in the U.S. today are totally dependent on government programs.
    - By 2035, 80% of the projected growth in federal spending as a share of GDP (other than interest payments on the debt) will come from growth in spending on the three largest entitlement programs: Medicare, Medicaid, and Social Security.
    - Unfunded entitlement programs approximate $53 Trillion.

- According to the Congressional Budgetary Office, in 2020, 47% of our Federal Budget will be comprised of Social Security, Medicare and Medicaid.
- Funding for Social Security benefits is projected to run out in 2017.

Sources: Congressional Budgetary Office and IRS.gov websites

2. Discretionary spending: funding that Congress must re-appropriate by vote each year.

3. Interest Payments: the annual costs associated with the federal debt. As the federal government runs deficits and borrows money, it builds up an accumulated level of debt. The government, just as any other borrower, has to pay interest on that debt.

   - The national debt as this chapter is written is $14 Trillion.
   - Projections indicate that in 2014 our federal deficit will be greater than our annual inflow.
   - Our national debt approximates to increase to nearly 100% of GDP by 2020.
   - Each year since 1969, Congress has overspent its income. The Treasury Department has to borrow money to meet Congress's appropriations. As taxpayers, we pay a staggering amount of interest on that huge debt. And now the Treasury is having trouble finding lenders! Soon the interest payment on your loan is bigger than any other item in your budget. Eventually, all you can do is pay the interest payment, and you don't have any money left over for anything else.

Switching gears now from your government's money to your household's money, let's turn to your personal wealth. There are four buckets of wealth:

1. Pre-tax: this refers to contributions made before paying income taxes, such as with a deductible IRA, SEP, 401k, PSP, etc.
2. After-tax: this refers to contributions or investments made after paying income taxes such as with a saving account, CD, mutual fund, etc.

3. Tax-deferred: this is income on which the payment of taxes is deferred until a later time, such as the unrecognized growth of an investment, or build-up of cash value of an annuity.
4. Tax Free: this is income on which no tax liability exists, such as qualified distributions from a Roth IRA, and other non-qualified assets such as properly structured withdrawals from life insurance. Note: Income from municipal bonds may be both federal and state income tax free, depending on the type. However while the income is income tax-free it may be included in the Alternative Minimum Tax (AMT) calculation.

The following example of the effect of taxation on your personal wealth is a commonly experienced scenario. One common sense rule of investing is to buy low, hold, and sell high, right? If you had invested $10 into the S&P 500 Index * in 1958; that $10 would have grown to $1100 in 2008. But after federal income taxes, that value would have shrunk 75% to $303. And that doesn't even include state, local, and consumption taxes. Are you evaluating net rate of return or gross rate of return? Are your current strategies designed to save you taxes or are you merely delaying the tax burden?

Will unexpected taxation affect your future standard of living? The wealth you may be counting on is wealth the government is counting on as well. Depending on which bucket of wealth holds the majority of your dollars, you may not wind up in the tax bracket you expected! Forward thinkers will seek out strategies to insulate themselves and their heirs from the massive tax liability facing all Americans.

Does the past offer us any insight into the future? The Federal Income Tax in its present form started in 1913 with a top tax bracket of 7% on income over $500,000. The highest tax bracket peaked in 1952-1953 at 92% tax on income over $400,000. The top tax bracket today starts with annual household income over $388,350 and is taxed at 35%. What's different now? Our national budget will force the hand of government once again. Though we cannot predict the exact actions of our future government, we can act now on solid data, strategies, and foresight to minimize the impact to our personal wealth.

---

* For illustrative purposes only. One may not invest directly into an index.

It's not all bad news; you are not powerless! Visit www.usdebtclock.org to raise your awareness and visit with your trusted financial advisor to seek solutions to these urgent and imminent problems. Actions taken now can help you to achieve the retirement and legacy you are working so hard to attain. You can enjoy the fruits of your labor by shielding your crops from the storms. Just don't wait until the sky darkens.

14

The Tax Train Is Coming: What are you going to do about it?

Planning for the next phase of your life is absolutely critical. Certainly none of us know exactly what is going to happen with all the financial variables involved. However, there are several considerations to evaluate:

1) Baby Boomers
   - As a demographic, Baby Boomers are staggeringly awful savers.
   - Half of the living (approximately seventy million) Baby Boomers are or will be dependent on Social Security, Medicare, and Medicaid.
   - Source: CBO & IRS.gov websites
2) Government Spending
   - It's almost impossible to avoid hearing about this subject these days as it's on every radio, television, and internet news outlet.
   - Bottom line: government spending is occurring at an astronomical level.
3) Tax Outcomes
   - We have a declining revenue base via Baby Boomers no longer earning income
   - We have an increasing expense/cost basis via Baby Boomers tapping into entitlement programs and government spending
   - Where do you think taxes will be in the future???

When evaluating strategy regarding these variables, let us consider first where you think taxes will end up when you are age sixty and seventy, i.e.

during your formative distribution years. The second item to consider is much like a flow-chart; based on your answer to question number one, where do you feel your assets should be positioned? Let's now spend some time discussing the various buckets of wealth; namely, what assets comprise them, and also, how are they treated from a tax perspective.

Specifically, you have two main buckets of money: taxable and tax-free. The following is what comprises each of these buckets.

Taxable:

Capital Gains

- Stocks
- Mutual Funds
- Sale of Business Interests
- Real Estate

Ordinary Income

- Wages
- Pre-tax retirement contributions
    - 401k & 403b
    - SEP & SIMPLE IRA

Tax-Free:

- Municipal Bonds
    - Income is exempt from Federal Income Tax, but may be subject to state and local taxes.
    - Bond value will fluctuate with market conditions, and bonds redeemed prior to maturity may be worth more or less than their original cost. Municipal bond income may also be subject to AMT (Alternative Minimum Tax).
- Roth IRA Qualified Distributions
    - It must occur at least five years after the Roth IRA owner established and funded his/her first Roth IRA
    - At least 59 ½ years old, $10k to first home, disability, at death
- Cash Value Life Insurance
    - Policy loans and withdrawals reduce the policy's cash value and death benefit and may result in a taxable event. Withdrawals

up to the basis paid into the contract and loans thereafter will not create an immediate taxable event, but substantial tax ramifications could result upon contract lapse or surrender. Surrender charges may reduce the policy's cash value in early years.

From a planning discussion, when we discuss money and financial objectives we look at four primary categories in the following order of importance.

1) Free Money: Inherited, Matching 401(k)
2) Tax-Free Money: Roth IRA, Life Insurance Cash Value (properly structured)
3) Tax-Deferred Money: Annuities, Qualified retirement plans (401(k), IRA, etc.)
4) Taxable Money: Wages, Capital gains, Interest

Where are your monies currently? Where do you feel you will receive the most bang for your buck? Our premise is, even though we feel strongly that tax brackets will be higher in the future, we still need to approach this holistically. Our friends in Congress have a propensity for changing policies, tax law, etc. As such, we need to evaluate our current needs, our ongoing objectives, and future goals comprehensively to arrive at a strategy which hedges as many outcomes as possible. Additionally, we need to ensure our plan is agile enough to change as our tax, legislative, and planning environment changes.

15

Life Insurance Tax Planning

What is tax planning with life insurance?

Life insurance can help you achieve various goals. Tax planning with life insurance involves minimizing the tax consequences of your life insurance decisions. Tax planning vehicles involving life insurance will vary, depending on the form of insurance coverage you select. In order to make informed insurance tax planning decisions, you must understand topics such as the tax-deferred buildup of cash value, the taxation of withdrawals, proceeds, loans, and dividends, and the deductibility of premiums. In addition, your insurance tax planning should involve a general understanding of the advantages and disadvantages of straight life insurance, modified endowment contracts, personal life insurance trusts, business use of life insurance, and life insurance as a part of a plan for charitable giving.

What is the tax-deferred buildup of cash value?

The cash value increase in an insurance policy resulting from investment income on premiums paid is not taxable income as long as the policy remains in force, even if the policy terminates in a death claim. Thus, the buildup (increase) of the cash value represents tax-deferred income.

What are the general tax rules for life insurance?

For federal income tax purposes, a life insurance contract in order to qualify for favorable tax treatment must meet applicable state law; either the *cash value accumulation test* (the net cash surrender value—the policy owner's current equity in the contract) cannot exceed the discounted value of the net single premium that could compound to the face amount of the policy at age 95. The discount factor is 4 percent, or the minimum rate guaranteed in the contract or the *guideline premium test* (The guideline premium is based upon the guideline single premium or the sum of the guideline level premiums to date.) The guideline-single-premium portion of the test limits the amount a policy owner may invest in a policy. You cannot pay more into a life insurance policy than the net present value of the future benefits to be paid at age 95 (the full face amount of the policy), discounted at 6 percent, assuming the contract's stated mortality and expenses. The guideline level premium refers to the level annual amount that will fund the future benefits (the face amount at age 95) payable to age 95, assuming the contract's stated mortality and expense charges and 4 percent interest. The cash-value corridor requirement refers to the percentage relationship of the policy's death benefit (face amount payable to beneficiary) to the policy owner's equity (the accumulated cash value of the policy's fixed and variable investment account assets).

The tax treatment of your life insurance policy will vary depending on the type of distribution i.e., a lifetime distribution, or death proceeds, or dividends. Generally speaking, lifetime distributions (other than loans) from such cash value life insurance policies are treated as made on a first in/first out (FIFO) basis for federal income tax purposes. In other words, money that you take out is treated as your nontaxable basis or investment in the contract first. Only amounts that exceed your basis are treated as taxable distributions.

Distributions

A lifetime distribution is any payment of the cash value of a life insurance policy during the lifetime of the insured, as opposed to the payment of the proceeds following the death of the insured. Generally, there are three major types of lifetime distributions: loans, partial surrenders, and full surrenders.

- With a loan, the policyowner borrows money from the insurance company, using the cash value of his or her policy as collateral to secure the loan. The amount of the loan balance reduces both the cash surrender value of the policy and the death proceeds until the loan is repaid. Policy loans generally do not generate immediate income tax liability for the policyowner because they are not treated as distributions for tax purposes. The loan proceeds are not included in taxable income as long your policy remains in force. However, if your policy lapses or you surrender the policy, you will be required to include the outstanding loan proceeds in gross income to the extent that the proceeds exceed your investment in the policy.

Example(s): Assume you have a life insurance policy as follows: cash value equals $15,000, owner's basis equals $14,000, and unrealized gain equals $1,000. If you borrow $15,000 from your life insurance policy, your unrealized gain of $1,000 will not be taxable at present. At your death, your insurance company will subtract any outstanding loan balance (plus interest) from the death proceeds and pay the remainder tax free to your beneficiary. (The issue date of the policy doesn't matter for loans.)

- In many cases, you may choose simply to withdraw and keep all or part of the cash value buildup in your policy. This is known as a partial surrender, which reduces the cash surrender value of the policy and the death benefit amounts. Generally, a partial surrender is taxed on a first in/first out (FIFO) basis. Thus, only amounts received in excess of your basis will be treated as taxable income.

- A full surrender occurs when you discontinue your policy. Typically, the insurance company sends you a check for the net cash surrender value at such a time. In terms of taxation, the excess of the cash surrender value of the policy (plus any outstanding loans) over your basis in the contract is treated as taxable income.

Death Proceeds

Generally, amounts you receive under a life insurance contract paid by reason of the death of the insured are not included in your gross income; such proceeds are received tax-free. Amounts payable on the death of the insured, whether these amounts represent return of premiums paid, the increased value of the policy due to investments, or the death benefit feature. It is immaterial whether the life insurance proceeds are received in a lump-sum or otherwise. However, any interest paid along with the life insurance proceeds is generally taxable.

Tip: It's also important to be aware of the estate and gift tax aspects of life insurance. In general, the proceeds of a policy are included in the estate of the insured if:

- The proceeds were payable to or for the benefit of the estate of the insured; or
- The policy was transferred by the decedent for less than fair consideration (value) within three years before his or her death; or
- The insured held any incidents of ownership at the time of death, such as the right to change the beneficiary.
- If you make a gift of your interest in a life insurance policy, the fair market value of your interest in the policy at the time of the gift may be subject to gift taxes.

Dividends

An insurance dividend is the amount of your premium that is paid back to you if your insurance company achieves a lower mortality cost on policyholders than it expected. Dividends on a life insurance policy are generally treated as a return of investment and are not treated as taxable income to the policyowner unless they exceed the amount of the aggregate gross premiums paid on the policy. It doesn't matter whether the dividends are received in cash or left with the insurance company to prepay premiums or to accumulate. If you leave these dividends on deposit with your insurance company and they earn interest, however, the interest you receive should be included as taxable interest income.

The premiums you pay for life insurance coverage are generally not deductible.

What about modified endowment contracts?

A modified endowment contract (MEC) is a special class of life insurance contract defined under the Internal Revenue Code (IRC). The IRC applies special tax rules to MECs. Generally speaking, loans and partial surrenders from MECs result in immediate taxation to the extent that the cash value of the contract exceeds the premiums paid. In addition, withdrawals and loans from a MEC before age 59 ½ may be subject to a 10 percent penalty.

What about personal life insurance trusts?

Sometimes it makes sense to either transfer an existing insurance policy on your life into a trust or to have a trust purchase a new insurance policy on your life. There are two types of trusts that can be used: an irrevocable life insurance trust (one that cannot be changed or revoked) or a revocable life insurance trust (one that can be changed or revoked). The tax treatment of these two types of trusts differs.

Irrevocable Life Insurance Trust

The main benefit to this type of trust is that after you die, the proceeds of the life insurance policy will not be included in your estate for estate tax purposes. Therefore, this type of trust is often used if your assets will exceed the applicable exclusion amount at the time of your death, or if you want to control the timing of a beneficiary's receipt of money. Another advantage to this trust is that if your trust beneficiaries are given Crummy powers (Note: a technique that enables a person to receive a gift not eligible for gift tax exclusion and change it into one that is. In order for this to work a gift must be stipulated as part of the trust when the trust is drafted and follow current limits among other estate tax requirements) your lifetime transfers of cash into the trust (to purchase a life insurance policy) may qualify for the annual exclusion from the gift tax.

Revocable Life Insurance Trust

Assets in a revocable life insurance trust must be included in your taxable estate when you die. This could create adverse estate tax consequences. Nevertheless, this type of trust can be useful if your beneficiaries are minor children and you want to control the timing of the receipt of the insurance proceeds.

Regarding business insurance, what are some of the planning vehicles?

Businesses often use several different types of insurance policies, and the tax treatment will vary depending on the type of policy. Life insurance in the form of group insurance, key employee coverage, split dollar, or corporate-owned policies can be used as an employee benefit and/or to accomplish certain business-related goals. In addition, property, casualty, and liability insurance policies are used to guard against disasters and lawsuits. Furthermore, insurance can be used to fund retirement plans and buy/sell agreements. If you are a business owner, then you may be concerned with both the deductibility of premiums and the taxation of proceeds.

In general, no deduction is allowed for premiums paid by a business on any life insurance policy covering the life of any officer or employee of the employer, or of any person financially interested in any trade or business carried on by the employer, when the employer is directly or indirectly a beneficiary under the policy. Typically, therefore, a business cannot deduct premiums paid on insurance policies used to fund buy/sell agreements and retirement plans. Also, premiums paid by a business on key employee coverage and split dollar life policies are also generally not deductible. However, a business can generally deduct the cost of group life coverage that it provides to its employees, as well as the cost of property, casualty, and liability insurance.

Despite the general lack of a deduction for premiums paid, life insurance can be a valuable tool for many businesses. Life insurance proceeds can usually be received tax-free. In addition, the cash value buildup on a life insurance policy is generally not taxed currently, although this buildup could cause the business to be subject to the alternative minimum tax (AMT) in certain situations. And the treatment of withdrawals and loans is often favorable.

In general, a business's withdrawals of cash value under a life insurance policy are treated as taxable distribution of earnings on the contract first. Withdrawals that exceed the business's earnings on the contract will be treated as a nontaxable recovery of basis in the contract. Loans, on the other hand, are not treated as distributions. Therefore, they are not subject to immediate taxation. In some cases, interest on policy loans may be deductible.

The deduction for casualty losses is treated differently for business purposes than for individual purposes. For tax purposes, a casualty means a loss of property that results from a fire, storm, shipwreck or other sudden catastrophe that causes direct damage. To the extent that the money or property a business receives as a reimbursement for a casualty loss is less than the adjusted basis of the property that was damaged, the business can deduct the full amount of the difference. However, no loss deduction will be allowed to the extent that such losses are covered by insurance coverage if the business decides not to file a claim.

How can tax planning with life insurance help you with charitable giving?

You may have a great desire to contribute to a favorite charity or charities. At the same time, you may be concerned about having sufficient assets remaining for your family members or other loved ones. Using life insurance as a part of your charitable giving strategy may allow you to accomplish both of the above goals and provide tax benefits to you as well.

Naming the charity as a beneficiary

If you name a charity as the beneficiary of your life insurance policy, the proceeds will not be a part of your taxable estate. Your estate will be entitled to an estate tax charitable deduction, but you will not be entitled to an income tax deduction. This strategy is appropriate if you want to maintain access to the policy's cash surrender value during your lifetime but want to leave the death benefit proceeds to charity.

Transferring policy ownership to charity

You can also transfer ownership of your life insurance policy to a charity or pay the premiums on life insurance policies owned by a charity. You may qualify for a limited income tax deduction if you meet the necessary qualifications. An outright gift of life insurance policy to charity is sheltered from gift tax by the gift tax charitable deduction.

Gift of cash surrender value

You cannot claim a gift tax charitable deduction if you assign only the cash surrender value of the policy to a charity and retain the rights to designate the beneficiary and assign the balance of the policy.

Tip: You can also use life insurance in conjunction with charitable reminder trusts: An arrangement in which property or money is donated to a charity, but the donor (called the grantor) continues to use the property and/or receive income from it while living. The beneficiaries receive the income and the charity receives the principal after a specified period of time. The grantor avoids any capital gains tax on the donated assets, and also gets an income tax deduction for the fair market value of the remainder interest that the trust earned. In addition, the asset is removed from the estate, reducing subsequent estate taxes. While the contribution is irrevocable, the grantor may have some control over the way the assets are invested, and may even switch from one charity to another (as long as it's still a qualified charitable organization). CRTs come in three types: charitable remainder annuity trust (which pays a fixed dollar amount annually), a charitable remainder unitrust (which pays a fixed percentage of the trust's value annually), and a charitable pooled income fund (which is set up by the charity, enabling many donors to contribute).

16

All about IRAs

An Individual Retirement Account (IRA) is a personal retirement savings plan that offers specific tax benefits. In fact, IRAs are one of the most powerful retirement savings tools available to you. Even if you're contributing to a 401(k) or other plan at work, you should also consider investing in an IRA. The following information and tables is primarily sourced from http://www.irs.gov/retirement/participant/article/0,,id=202518,00.html.

What types of IRAs are available?

There are two major types of IRAs: traditional IRAs and Roth IRAs. Both allow you to make annual contributions of up to $5,000 as of the printing of this book. Generally, you must have at least as much taxable compensation as the amount of your IRA contribution. But if you are married filing jointly, your spouse can also contribute to an IRA, even if he or she does not have taxable compensation. The law also allows taxpayers age 50 and older to make additional "catch-up" contributions. These folks can put up to $6,000 in their IRAs.

Both traditional and Roth IRAs feature tax-sheltered growth of earnings. And both give you a wide range of investment choices. However, there are important differences between these two types of IRAs. You must understand these differences before you can choose the type of IRA that's best for you.

Traditional IRAs

Practically anyone can open and contribute to a traditional IRA. The only requirements are that you must have taxable compensation and be under age 70½. You can contribute the maximum allowed each year as long as your taxable compensation for the year is at least that amount. If your taxable compensation for the year is below the maximum contribution allowed, you can contribute only up to the amount you earned. Note: MAGI = Modified Adjusted Gross Income.

Tax Year 2012 **Individuals Covered by an Employer Plan**		
Filing status	**Deduction is limited if MAGI between:**	**No deduction if MAGI over:**
Single/Head of household	*$58,000-$68,000*	*$68,000*
Married joint*	*$92,000-$112,000*	*$112,000*
Married separate	*$0-$10,000*	*$10,000*
* If you are not covered by an employer sponsored retirement plan, but your spouse is, your deduction is eliminated if your MAGI is $173,000 to $183,000.		

Your contributions to a traditional IRA may be tax deductible on your federal income tax return. This is important because tax-deductible (pre-tax) contributions lower your taxable income for the year, saving you money in taxes. If neither you nor your spouse is covered by a 401(k) or other employer-sponsored plan, you can generally deduct the full amount of your annual contribution. If one of you is covered by such a plan, your ability to deduct your contributions depends on your annual income MAGI and your income tax filing status. You may qualify for a full deduction, a partial deduction, or no deduction at all.

What happens when you start taking money from your traditional IRA? Any portion of a distribution that represents deductible contributions is subject to income tax because those contributions were not taxed when you made them. Any portion that represents investment earnings is also subject to income tax because those earnings were not previously taxed either. Only the portion that represents nondeductible, after-tax contributions (if any) is not subject to income tax. In addition to income tax, you may have to pay a 10% early withdrawal penalty if you're under age 59½, unless you meet one of the exceptions:

- You have reached age 59½ by the time of the withdrawal
- The withdrawal is made because of disability

- The withdrawal is made to pay first-time homebuyer expenses ($10,000 lifetime limit from all IRAs)
- The withdrawal is made by your beneficiary or estate after your death

If you wish to defer taxes, you can leave your funds in the traditional IRA, but only until April 1 of the year following the year you reach age 70½. That's when you have to take your first required minimum distribution from the IRA. After that, you must take a distribution by the end of every calendar year until your funds are exhausted or you die. The annual distribution amounts are based on a standard life expectancy table. You can always withdraw more than you're required to in any year. However, if you withdraw less, you'll be hit with a 50% penalty on the difference between the required minimum and the amount you actually withdrew.

Roth IRAs

Not everyone can set up a Roth IRA. Even if you can, you may not qualify to take full advantage of it. The first requirement is that you must have taxable compensation. If your taxable compensation is at least $5,000 in 2012, you may be able to contribute the full amount. But it becomes more complicated. Your ability to contribute to a Roth IRA in any year depends on your MAGI and your income tax filing status. Your allowable contribution may be less than the maximum possible, or nothing at all.

Tax Year 2012		
Filing status	**Contribution is limited if MAGI between:**	**No contribution if MAGI over:**
Single/Head of household	$110,000-$125,000	$125,000
Married joint	$173,000-$183,000	$183,000
Married separate	$0-$10,000	$10,000

Your contributions to a Roth IRA are not tax deductible. You can invest only after-tax dollars in a Roth IRA. The good news is, if you meet certain conditions, your withdrawals from a Roth IRA will be completely free from federal income tax, including both contributions and investment earnings. To be eligible for these qualifying distributions, you must meet a five-year holding period requirement. In addition, one of the following must apply:

- You have reached age 59½ by the time of the withdrawal
- The withdrawal is made because of disability
- The withdrawal is made to pay first-time homebuyer expenses ($10,000 lifetime limit from all IRAs)
- The withdrawal is made by your beneficiary or estate after your death

Qualifying distributions will also avoid the 10% early withdrawal penalty. This ability to withdraw your funds with no taxes or penalty is a key strength of the Roth IRA. And remember, even nonqualifying distributions will be taxed (and possibly penalized) only on the investment earnings portion of the distribution, and then only to the extent that your distribution exceeds the total amount of all contributions that you have made.

Note: In 2010, the income limits for conversions to a Roth IRA were repealed. As such, if you have either monies from a previous employer's retirement plan or a rollover IRA you are eligible to convert those dollars to a Roth IRA. Another strategy to consider is to fund a non-deductible IRA (no tax break today) and subsequently convert those monies to a Roth IRA in effect deploying a 'back-door' Roth IRA. We encourage you to consult with your CPA or Tax Advisor to determine if this strategy is appropriate for you as the conversion may generate taxes.

Another advantage of the Roth IRA is that there are no required distributions after age 70½ or at any time during your life. You can put off taking distributions until you really need the income. Or, you can leave the entire balance to your beneficiary without ever taking a single distribution. Also, as long as you have taxable compensation and qualify, you can keep contributing to a Roth IRA after age 70½.

Choose the right IRA for you.

Assuming you qualify to use both, which type of IRA is best for you? Sometimes the choice is easy. The Roth IRA will probably be a more effective tool if you don't qualify for tax-deductible contributions to a traditional IRA. However, if you can deduct your traditional IRA contributions, the choice is more difficult. Most professionals believe that a Roth IRA will still give you more value for your dollars in the long run, but it depends on your personal goals and circumstances. The Roth IRA may very well make more sense if you want to minimize taxes during retirement and preserve assets for your beneficiaries. A traditional deductible IRA may be a better tool if you want to lower your yearly tax bill while you're still working. A financial professional or tax advisor can help you pick the right type of IRA for you.

Note: *You can have both a traditional IRA and a Roth IRA, but your total annual contribution to all of the IRAs that you own cannot be more than $5,000 ($6,000 if you're age 50 or older).*

17

Active vs. Passive Portfolio Management

One of the longest-standing debates in investing is over the relative merits of active portfolio management versus passive management. With an actively managed portfolio, a manager tries to beat the performance of a given benchmark index by using his or her judgment in selecting individual securities and deciding when to buy and sell them. A passively managed portfolio attempts to match that benchmark performance, and in the process, minimize expenses that can reduce an investor's net return.

Each camp has strong advocates who argue that the advantages of its approach outweigh those for the opposite side.

Active Investing: attempting to add value

Proponents of active management believe that by picking the right investments, taking advantage of market trends, and attempting to manage risk, a skilled investment manager can generate returns that outperform a benchmark index. For example, an active manager whose benchmark is the Standard & Poor's 500 Index (S&P 500) might attempt to earn better-than-market returns by overweighting certain industries or individual securities, allocating more to those sectors than the index does. Or a manager might try to control a portfolio's overall risk by temporarily increasing the percentage devoted to more conservative investments, such as cash alternatives.

An actively managed individual portfolio also permits its manager to take tax considerations into account. For example, a separately managed account can harvest capital losses to offset any capital gains realized by its owner, or time a sale to minimize any capital gains. An actively managed mutual fund can do the same on behalf of its collective shareholders.

However, an actively managed mutual fund's investment objective will put some limits on its manager's flexibility; for example, a fund may be required to maintain a certain percentage of its assets in a particular type of security. A fund's prospectus will outline any such provisions, and you should read it before investing.

Passive Investing: focusing on costs

Advocates of unmanaged passive investing, sometimes referred to as indexing, have long argued that the best way to capture overall market returns is to use low-cost market-tracking index investments. This approach is based on the concept of the efficient market, which states that because all investors have access to all the necessary information about a company and its securities, it's difficult if not impossible to gain an advantage over any other investor. As new information becomes available, market prices adjust in response to reflect a security's true value. That market efficiency, proponents say, means that reducing investment costs is the key to improving net returns.

Indexing does create certain cost efficiencies. Because the investment simply reflects an index, no research is required for securities selection. Also, because trading is relatively infrequent—passively managed portfolios typically buy or sell securities only when the index itself changes—trading costs often are lower. Also, infrequent trading typically generates fewer capital gains distributions, which means relative tax efficiency.

Popular investment choices that use passive management are index funds and exchange-traded funds (ETFs). However, some actively managed ETFs are now being introduced, and index funds and ETFs can be used as part of an active manager's strategy.

Note: *Before investing in either an active or passive ETF or mutual fund, carefully consider the investment objectives, risks, charges, and expenses, which can be found in the prospectus available from the fund. Read it carefully before investing.*

Active Management	Passive Management
Attempts to beat benchmark performance	Attempts to match benchmark performance
Contends pricing inefficiencies in the market create investing opportunities	Contends that it is difficult or impossible to "beat the market"
Securities selected by portfolio manager	Securities selected based on an index
Focuses on choice of specific securities and timing of trades	Focuses on overall sector or asset class
Trading and the degree of liquidity for individual securities may increase portfolio costs	Infrequent trading tends to minimize portfolio expenses

Blending Approaches with Asset Allocation

The core/satellite approach represents one way to have the best of both worlds. It is essentially an asset allocation model that seeks to resolve the debate about indexing versus active portfolio management. Instead of following one investment approach or the other, the core/satellite approach blends the two. The bulk, or "core," of your investment dollars are kept in cost-efficient passive investments designed to capture market returns by tracking a specific benchmark. The balance of the portfolio is then invested in a series of "satellite" investments, in many cases actively managed, which typically have the potential to boost returns and lower overall portfolio risk.

Bear in mind, however, that no investment strategy can assure a profit or protect against losses.

Controlling Investment Costs

Devoting a portion rather than the majority of your portfolio to actively managed investments can allow you to minimize investment costs that may reduce returns.

For example, consider a hypothetical $400,000 portfolio that is 100% invested in actively managed mutual funds with an average expense level of 1.5%, which results in annual expenses of $6,000. If 70% of the portfolio were invested instead in a low-cost index fund or ETF with an average expense level of .25%, annual expenses on that portion of the portfolio would run $700 per year. If a series of satellite investments with expense ratios of 2% were used for the remaining 30% of the portfolio, annual expenses on the satellites would be $2,400. Total annual fees for both core and satellites would total $3,100, producing savings of $2,900 per year. Reinvested in the portfolio, that amount could increase its potential long-term growth. (This hypothetical portfolio is intended only as an illustration of the math involved rather than the results of any specific investment, of course.)

Popular core investments often track broad benchmarks such as the S&P 500, the Russell 2000® Index, the NASDAQ 100, and various international and bond indices. Other popular core investments may track specific style or market-capitalization benchmarks in order to provide a value versus growth bias or a market capitalization tilt.

While core holdings generally are chosen for their low-cost ability to closely track a specific benchmark, satellites are generally selected for their potential to add value, either by enhancing returns or by reducing portfolio risk. Here, too, you have many options. For example, satellite investments might include hedge funds, private equity, real estate, stocks of emerging companies, or sector funds, to name only a few. Good candidates for satellite investments include less efficient asset classes where the potential for active management to add value is increased. That is especially true for asset classes whose returns are not closely correlated with the core or with other satellite investments. Since it's not uncommon for satellite investments to be more volatile than the core, it's important to always view them within the context of the overall portfolio.

III

Protect Your Wealth

18

Asset Protection Considerations

Asset protection laws are determined by each state. The first step is to visit with a financial advisor and local counsel to evaluate the legal ramifications of using various investments or business arrangements. In some states, the investment vehicle itself has been provided with asset protection features under the state statutes. In other instances, you may consider implementing legal entities such as an LLC, LLP, FLP, FST, PA, or PC. Depending on the client circumstances, structuring asset protection vehicles outside the country might be considered. It is critical to consult an attorney licensed in your state of residence who is experienced in this area of the law, to assist you in determining which strategy is appropriate for you and ensure that appropriate tax filings are made.

We are delighted to introduce Ike Devji, an attorney specializing in asset protection. The following is an excerpt from his nationally publicized article about asset protection which he kindly has given us permission to provide to you.

Asset Protection 101—Basics Every Doctor Must Know

Good financial advisors seek to create safe, steady growth and help you avoid losses and exposures to things like market risk and income and estate taxes. A natural extension of that stewardship is making sure that the growth you are fostering, as well as the balance of your assets, are safe from exposure to an increasingly predatory and hostile litigation system. Not only is litigation against doctors more common than ever (as is evidenced by the heated debate on this topic in the context of our national healthcare debate), it's more dangerous than ever given the multiple attacks on the wealth of the thousands of doctors we serve including:

- Current Economic Conditions
- Decreasing Compensation and Insurance Reimbursement Rates
- Increasingly Hostile Litigation System that Targets YOUR wealth
- Stalled or Negative Investment Momentum
- Increasing Overhead and Liability Insurance Costs
- Decreases in Liability Insurance Protection due to large awards, *consent to settle* and *defense inside the limits* clauses in your current coverage
- Increasing Employee Lawsuit exposure; suits against medical employers have tripled in the last ten years!
- Increasing burdens of Income and Estate Taxes; the death tax will be 55% of everything over $1MM in 2011 as of the time of publication

Most of our clients have obvious exposures, such as a physician's potential malpractice exposure or the enduring liability that a large commercial contractor faces. Other sources of exposure are more insidious, such as merely being wealthy and visible, owning income property, or something as simple as you (or your kids) owning and driving a car every day. The numbers are staggering; we are at a point in our litigation system where we have *over 70,000 lawsuits filed per day in the United States alone*, many without any real merit. Unfortunately being "right" or careful is not enough to keep you safe, nor is relying on your skill and experience.

What we and our clients must take to heart is that litigation attorneys are in *business*. Just like any business, including yours, they have weekly meetings in which they examine growth, cash flow, revenue goals and new leads or opportunities. This economic motivation is a key and explains in part why we see awards rising and why plaintiffs' attorneys regularly seek and obtain awards above the limits of applicable liability insurance policies. The average medical malpractice *policy*, as just one example, is $1MM, whereas the average national malpractice *award* is about $3.9 million. This leaves the physician "holding the bag" for the other several million dollars. The average doctor simply can't survive that kind of a loss and maintain their financial goals.

Why are your advisors concerned?

As illustrated by the numbers below, awards continue to spiral out of control, fueled by litigation attorneys who have become partners in lawsuits and who are economically incentivized to create and magnify adversarial relations between parties who might otherwise reach some reasonable, if not amicable, settlement.

WHAT ESTABLISHES THE NEED FOR ASSET PROTECTION?

Facts about our litigation system for you:

- We live in a society that files some 70,000 lawsuits per day, many without merit;
- The average medical malpractice award is $3.9 MM, some authorities put this number substantially higher;
- The average legal costs of settling a frivolous lawsuit is $91,000—plus the actual settlement amount itself;
- The average sexual harassment suit against a small business produces a verdict of $530,000. Employees are suing more often, winning more often and winning proportionally larger judgments. They win 75% of the time;
- Only the top 5% of Americans has a net worth of over $1MM. Using that as a baseline, it's pretty easy to see where even a client who is worth only a few million dollars fits in on the food chain.

COMMON RISK FACTORS OF OUR CLIENTS—some combination of any of the following:

- They are high net-worth, high liability, or they will be soon (i.e. new doctor)
- They are highly visible, traceable, and or collectible
- They have assets that would be difficult to replace if lost or reduced
- They have employees
- They own their own business
- They have professional liability
- They own liability generating assets, i.e. rental property

- They have children

Can't we just insure our way to safety?

No, unfortunately, for a number of reasons:

First, it's impossible to insure yourself against every possible contingency and exposure. There will always be many exposures for which no insurance exists or which are not adequately covered by the amount of coverage the client has in place or can afford.

Second, the liability insurance business model is simple: take lots of premiums in and pay as few claims as possible. The difference equals profit. When an insured contacts their own carrier to report a claim, a number of the questions asked by the insurance company seek to determine if coverage can be reduced or excluded due to the contributory negligence of their own insured. Think about these questions: "Were you wearing your seatbelt? Were you smoking or on your cell phone at the time of your accident? Do you wear corrective lenses? Had you ingested drugs or alcohol within the previous twenty-four hours?"

Third, the holy grail of the "umbrella policy" and policy limits are rarely fully understood by clients and advisors. To the consumer, "umbrella" means "everything". To the insurance company, it means specific occurrences to specific limits under specific conditions. Add to that the fact that many liability insurance policies are inclusive of defense costs and the actual amount left for the award is reduced, again exposing the insured person personally. For example, your physician or small business owner client has a $1 million liability policy in place and gets sued. The insurance company spends $400 thousand on defense costs and losses, resulting in an award of $1.2 million. In this scenario, only $600 thousand is available from the policy to put towards the claim itself.

Our advice: buy as much insurance as you can afford, assume it won't work and have a good back up plan.

A little proactive medicine goes a long way.

We are all aware that there is a ton of ***offense*** out there. You can't drive across town without seeing ads for contingency fee attorneys plastered on billboards, bus stops and without hearing their ads on the radio: "Were you injured at no fault of your own? Have you been treated unfairly at work? Did you take a medication that may have injured you? Call us; we will get you compensated at no cost to you". An interesting experiment is to Google "personal injury" along with the name of your city. The number of listings for attorneys will be staggering to you, especially when you consider that all those attorneys are in their offices right now waiting for the phone to ring, or thinking of ways to *make* it ring. Remember *your wealth* is the product that they sell and advertise.

The question is what kind of ***defensive planning*** have you examined? You insure your homes, cars, personal property, health and even your very life, but what level of planning and forethought have you invested in *insuring your net worth*? Typically very little forethought, other than liability insurance, has gone into this area. This lack of planning can be disastrous, especially for clients who have reached the pinnacle of their career and who are looking towards retirement. What option would a 58 year old doctor have if he or she lost a substantial portion of their net worth to a car accident in which there was a fatality, because their child had a party and another teenager died or was injured, or because they were accused of sexual harassment by a disgruntled employee (all issues I've addressed for clients recently)? Think you or your localities are immune? Just turn on the nightly news and realize that every fatal accident you see reported that day will likely be accompanied by a seven figure lawsuit.

A great deal of the defensive planning involves the proper titling and compartmentalization of assets into acceptable and easily manageable units of risk. It's easier than it sounds but still needs experienced guidance. The mantras we teach our clients are simple:

1. Own nothing, control everything;
2. What you don't own can't be taken from you;
3. The best defense is being an uncollectible target, take steps to remove the economic incentive to pursue you.

As is illustrated below, moving the title of assets to various appropriate and legitimate entities can dramatically reduce the amount of the exposure you face, and can actually help make the liability insurance you have in place more effective. How? It removes the economic incentive to pursue you beyond the limits of the policy and forces settlements into a reasonable range. Why pursue someone for more than the limits of their policy through a long and expensive court proceeding if they didn't have any assets that can be reached? For the plaintiff's attorney this is a losing proposition and he will likely encourage his client to settle so that he can move on to the next case after taking his share of the award.

In most cases, collectible assets can be sheltered or reduced by over 90% with the use of well tested and established tools like LLCs, Limited Partnerships, Asset Protection Trusts and Receivables and Income Protection plans, to name just a few examples.

The Value of Asset Protection

Before Asset Protection—Exposed

Home	*$1 Million Equity—own name*
2nd Home	*$500,000 Equity—own name*
Office	*$375,000 Equity—in RLT (Revocable Living Trust)*
Cash	*$100,000—own name*
Securities	*$500,000—in RLT*
Art & Jewelry	*$275,000—own name*
Receivables	*$2 Million—in single member LLC*
Personal Checking	*$50,000—own name*
Insurance Cash	*$1 Million—own name*
Qualified Plan	*$400,000—in Plan Name*

Results:	***Net Worth***	***Collectible***
	$6,650,000	***$6,250,000***

The Value of Asset Protection

After Asset Protection - Protected

Home	*$1 Million Equity—in Asset Protection Trust (A.P. Trust)*
2nd Home	*$500,000 Equity—in A.P. Trust*
Office	*$375,000 Equity—in LLC Owned by FLP (Family Limited Partnership)*
Cash	*$100,000—in FLP*
Securities	*$500,000—in FLP*
Art & Jewelry	*$275,000—in FLP*
Receivables	*$2 Million—in AR (Accounts Receivable) Program*
Personal Checking	*$50,00—own name*
Insurance Cash	*$1 Million—in AR Program*
Qualified Plan	*$400,000—in Plan Name*

Results:	***Net Worth***	***Collectible***
	$6,650,000	***$50,000***

As you can see, the vast majority of a client's collectible assets are accounted for and sheltered in this example. The best tools used are legal, tax neutral and have a legitimate business purpose. The numbers scale easily up or down.

I already have a "Revocable Living Trust". Doesn't this make me safe?

No, this is a dangerous misconception that the majority of the public is working under. The Revocable Living Trust or RLT is a wonderful estate planning tool. However, like most tools it has a specific purpose; in this case, primarily the avoidance of probate and estate taxes. The RLT is, as the first word in the title suggests, REVOCABLE during your lifetime. This means that during your lifetime you can easily be ordered to revoke the trust and tender trust assets for the payment of a judgment by a court.

This is a common occurrence. *The trust becomes irrevocable only upon your death.* Thus, during your lifetime it does not shelter you from any sort of lawsuit exposure. Conversely, Asset Protection does not replace or duplicate good estate planning, but rather works in conjunction with it.

What exactly can be protected?

Non-qualified investments, cash, stocks, both personal and investment or commercial real estate, business equipment, intellectual property, interests in non-liability generating businesses, valuable collections such as art and cars and even future income and business receivables are just a few examples. We typically exclude the personal checking accounts, personal "daily driver vehicles" and personal property.

Some Basics of Good Asset Protection Planning

1. **Do something today.** Asset Protection is like Net Worth Insurance. You can't insure against a loss after it's already happened. The only good attack against a properly drafted Asset Protection Plan is timing—that it was done too late and with the intent to "delay, hinder or defraud" a specific plaintiff.
2. **Be realistic about the possibility of exposure and about the effect that a six or seven figure judgment would have upon the financial plan you have in place.** The most common and egregious mistake made by advisors of all types is telling clients who are worth "only" a few million dollars, or who are working hard to get there, that they are not "big enough" to justify doing this kind of planning; this is nonsense. Of course a client worth five or ten or even $100 million needs this type of planning. But who will be affected more? The ten million dollar client can take a hit for a million or two and keep the cars, house, lifestyle and the kids in college, but our more average client would be financially devastated. *They need it even more.* Some of the smartest clients we have are typically new physicians with little more than six figures in student debt, a leased car and an apartment. Why? Because they understand that every day that passes strengthens the tools they have in place: "the longer it cooks, the harder the shell". They also know that they need to have a safe place *to put* every dollar

they make, have a safe place *within which* it can grow and *from which* to re-invest it and put it to work for their family.

3. **Have Top Counsel In Place In Three Core Areas: Asset Protection, Financial Management and Accounting**. A good team will help nurture your success, help protect you from loss, mistakes and scams and make sure that you get to keep the money you earn in a legal, efficient and ethical way. These team members make sure that you keep a larger portion of every dollar you make, pay as little in tax as the law allows and that your money works as hard for you as you did to get it.
4. **Use the right tools**. Asset Protection is part art, part science, just like your business. There are certain proven methods and tools that work and others that do not. Be wary of promoters, do it yourself kits and promises of domestic jurisdictions that will make you safe and save you money on taxes. Each tool has a specific business purpose that protects specific types of property, they are not all interchangeable.
5. **No, Nevada Corporations do not work**. In fact, they are increasingly viewed as presumptively fraudulent due to a long history of abuse and tax fraud. Thousands of consumers have purchased them under false promises of secrecy, bearer share anonymity and tax advantages. Almost all these promises are completely fictional. Our information shows us that the term "bearer shares" does not even exist in the statutes of the state of Nevada. Unless you live there, do business primarily from or in the state of Nevada and have the assets in question housed in the state, a Nevada LLC will not help you, especially if it lacks a real business purpose as explained below.
6. **Maintain a legitimate business purpose for all legal tools**. We commonly see good tools misused by clients and inexperienced planners which do more harm than good. In order to take advantage of the full protection the law affords we must maintain an essential business purpose for the tools we use. The use of limited partnerships for investment management and LLCs to hold investment or commercial real estate are two examples of well proven and tested business usages.
7. **No, transfers to a spouse, child or relative are not effective**. This is especially true if the transfer is made after an exposure has

occurred. A thinly disguised "gift" will easily be reversed and the property seized by the court in the event of a judgment. Further, these types of transfers are rarely legitimized by the appropriate recording and tax reporting formalities. If you gave your 17 year old your $1 million home at full equity, you better have a gift tax return illustrating that, and it better have been done well in advance of the harm complained of. Even if the gift is effectively made, all you have done is given away something you want to protect and exposed it to *another person's* liability.

8. **"Just" an S-corp. or an LLC is not enough.** Single member or closely held corporations with just one or two owners are exactly the type of entity you commonly hear referred to when you hear the phrase "piercing the corporate veil". If a business has only one or two owners who closely manage and control the operations of the business on a daily basis, or even worse, which are also directly responsible for a harm or injury, it is relatively simple for a court to pierce the veil and grant access to the owner's personal assets. This is especially true with successful small businesses and family businesses that often don't maintain the formalities of keeping personal and business expenditures completely separate, bolstering the argument that the person and the corporation are one and the same.
9. **Get professional, individual help**. There are a wide variety of skill levels in every profession, including the law. Many so-called Asset Protection professionals are not attorneys, or are attorneys who apply bits and pieces of knowledge from other fields of practice that may actually diminish legal protections in existence. Every plan must be uniquely tailored to the individual, their activities and the unique nature of their assets. There is no one-size-fits-all solution, even though clients with similar assets may have similar looking plans.
10. **The legal tools used are typically tax neutral**. Don't try to combine tax planning and Asset Protection. In most cases, the tools used are tax neutral and do not provide tax advantage or tax liability. Many times abusive tax structures are disguised as Asset Protection, often promising tax free growth offshore in various trusts or captive insurance plans. Putting money into a plan tax

free, growing it tax free and pulling it out tax free is rarely if ever possible; you can't have all three.

11. **Don't forget about income and receivables—protect the source.** Very often we see doctors that are concerned about protecting everything they have been fortunate enough to accumulate while ignoring ways to protect their future income. We find that many doctors, even those with a very high net worth, often have fixed business and personal overhead commitments based on the expectation of a certain income level. If they suddenly had that cash flow tap turned off, they would not be able to sustain their current monthly expenditures. This scenario would force them into a situation where they were selling off assets or going into qualified plans early and making substantial lifestyle changes. There are options available for qualified physicians that can securitize that income stream.
12. **Don't draw liability in.** In many cases physicians unintentionally escalate their value as a target. For instance, how many of your peers have vehicles that they or their spouse drive titled in the name of their business? Which of the following three defendants is most exciting to a plaintiff: John Smith, Dr. John Smith, or Smith Surgical Inc.? As you can see, the corporate defendant is often the most exciting and deepest pocket. In order to fix this we simply transfer the vehicle back to the client's name and have them take a car allowance from the business. Remember, with a good plan in place you won't have substantial exposed assets anyway.
13. **Have Adequate Levels of Insurance** on everything: malpractice liability, auto, home, life, long term care and disability. Buy every dollar of liability coverage you can afford, assume it won't be fully adequate and have a back-up plan.
14. **Protect your credit; it is one of your most enduring and valuable assets.** As credit markets have tightened, even the wealthy are having trouble obtaining credit for every day issues like home and auto purchase or leasing. This means check your credit reports regularly and take steps to protect your identity.

We are delighted to have a member on our team with Ike's expertise contribute to our book. Keep in mind, this introduction is just that, an introduction to the most basic concepts behind legal and effective Asset Protection planning and provides only generally applicable rules and issues to be aware of. When you are ready to explore the solutions available, we strongly encourage you to seek qualified counsel that has a proven record of experience in this specific field.

19

Disability Insurance Coverage

Most individuals take the time to insure their homes, autos, boat, and other tangible assets against loss. Many fail to realize that their ability to earn an income is the most significant asset they have. If you lose the ability to work, due to an accident or long-term illness, your income will stop, yet your expenses for yourself and your family continues. Protecting your income in the event of a long-term disability should not be overlooked when addressing your financial security.

Disability Insurance coverage can be used to address this risk. Some policy features to consider:

- Disability policies may be issued on an individual or group basis.
- Individual Policies are also available through associations and professional organizations not available to the public.
- Benefit periods can vary from 24 month, 60 months, to age 65 or age 67. The longer period is recommended in most cases.
- "Non-cancelable" and "guaranteed renewable" are important provisions to look for in a disability income policy. These provisions mean that the insurance company cannot raise your rates or discontinue your coverage as long as you continue to pay your premiums.
- Elimination or waiting periods typically range from 30 days to one year. This is the length of time you must wait until policy benefits are paid. Longer elimination periods result in lower premium cost.
- Cost of living adjustments protect against inflation.
- Future benefits based on income only (not medical) are highly beneficial.

- The definition of disability is covered later in more detail.

Other types of Disability Income Insurance policies include:

- Key Employee Disability Insurance—an employer may own a policy issued on a key employee. If the key employee becomes disabled, the policy benefits can be used to pay expenses related to the loss of services of that employee, such as hiring a replacement.
- Disability Buy-out—if a business owner or professional becomes disabled, these policy benefits can be used to satisfy the buy-out provisions of a buy/sell agreement.
- Business Overhead Expense—if a business owner or professional becomes disabled, it may be difficult to keep the business or practice running without their involvement. This type of policy can be used to provide funds to pay the on-going expense of the business (including temporary "stand-in" doctor salary), so it can continue functioning during a period of disability.

Of Special Note: There are many differences in policy provisions between different insurers and even between different contract forms from the same provider. Some policies do not require a complete disability, but pay benefits when an insured's earnings drop by a certain percentage due to a disability. Some providers require a physician's certification to pay or to continue paying benefits. There are policies that provide for partial or residual benefits; for example, where the insured is not able to perform all the duties of his/her profession, but could perform some duties. Policy definitions and provisions should be carefully reviewed to ensure your policy will meet your financial needs and circumstances.

The key to private disability insurance is identifying your most valuable asset. In this case, think about an asset bigger than your home, car, or your financial statements. You are your most valuable asset, specifically, your skill set, which ultimately provides your ability to earn income. You have worked very hard for many years getting to this point. The last thing you would want to happen is to become disabled without proper coverage, causing you to forfeit the income for which you have worked so hard.

A. *Definitions*

There are a variety of different definitions, so we will list the most common here.

- **"Specialty Specific" (also may be called Double Dip Own Occupation and "True Own Occupation").** Disability is defined as a condition which prevents you from performing the material and substantial duties of your specialty. Even if you are able to work in another capacity, you will still collect the disability income as a nonworking specialist *in addition to* the income from the other job. This applies regardless of whether or not your new job is in medicine.
- **"Transitional Occupation":** Like the previous type, if you cannot perform the material and substantial duties of your specialty you are considered disabled. However, if you earn an income, your total disability benefit will be proportionally reduced based on the amount of income earned from the new job (total new income disability benefit not to exceed previous earned income).
- **"Own Occupation" or "Regular Occupation"**: Again, if you cannot perform the material and substantial duties of your specialty you are considered disabled. You will only collect your disability benefit so long as you do NOT earn any income AND are under the constant care and supervision of a physician.

In our opinion, "Specialty Specific / Double Dip Own Occupation" disability coverage is the strongest definition and will best protect you and your family. Of course, it will still be important to evaluate which type of coverage is most appropriate for you. For instance, some contracts feature the "double dip own occupation" benefit for a limited time, usually between 24 and 60 months. Statistics indicate that if you are disabled for a period of two years or longer, you will most likely suffer ongoing disability for the remainder of your life. This is why a limited time frame for this benefit is not recommended in most cases.

B. *Cost*

The cost, or premium, will vary as it depends on your specialty, gender, health, age, and the various options you might elect to add to your coverage. Additionally there are affordable options included graded premiums and step-up provisions providing a lower initial cost increasing over time. If you have a plan for financial independence achieved within the break-even period this may be appropriate for you.

C. *Benefit Amount*

Another consideration is the amount of benefit you can actually receive. Often this requires combining policies from two or three companies in order to maximize the benefit. For example, some companies will offer $10,000 or $15,000 per month in benefit but will participate, or allow you to get additional coverage from other carriers in addition to what they offer, up to $50,000.

D. *Timing*

If you are in training, you should consider purchasing private disability insurance prior to entering practice. Consider these compelling reasons:

- While in training you can receive discounts on your premiums. This discount often carries forward, applying to future increases of benefit. Over time, this could amount to a significant savings for you.
- As is true with all insurance, premiums are based on age. The younger you are, the less risk you present to the insurer, hence lower premiums. People often ask how much of a premium increase they can expect by waiting one year or more to begin coverage. Typically premiums increase considerably with as little as one year delay of acquisition.
- Another variable is the possibility of being offered group disability coverage upon entering practice. Besides being chosen and controlled by someone else, group coverage often has more limited definitions, such as "Any Occupation." In other words, if you relied on this type of group disability coverage, and due to disability could not perform your specialty but could work at any other job, you would not be considered disabled and would not receive any benefits.

- Key Point: If you have private coverage in training, and upon employment, your group offers you disability coverage; your group coverage will stack on top of your private coverage. This ultimately covers a higher percentage of your income. If you wait and take the group coverage and then decide to purchase private coverage, the private carrier will likely provide very little, if any, in the way of extra coverage as they will say you already have 60% of your income covered by the group policy. This is why it is imperative to purchase private disability insurance prior to joining a group. One strategy we utilize for our clients already in practice is to determine if they can opt out of their group coverage. This way they can obtain the private policy that will cover a higher percentage of their income. Finally, the reality is that for many of you, the group you join immediately out of training will not be the group with whom you practice for the remainder of your career. For all of these reasons, relying on group disability insurance is a risky proposition.

E. *One final note about disability insurance . . .*

The disability insurance industry has undergone massive changes in the past twenty years. Some of your older colleagues likely have private disability insurance that would replace 100% of their income for the rest of their lives. Most new policies replace 50-60% of your income until you reach age 65 or 67. We know of only one company still offering lifetime benefits, and at a much higher cost than in the past. Since industry changes are rarely in favor of the insured, it is recommended that you acquire the maximum benefit as soon as possible.

20

Life Insurance Coverage

There are many different types of life insurance to consider. Because evaluating life insurance involves a variety of components, we will discuss an approach you may take in evaluating and purchasing life insurance, as well as review the various types of life insurance available.

Due to the various types of policies, each with a different approach to fulfilling one's needs for life insurance, it is important to evaluate and choose carefully. Key considerations include:

- Duration of the need
- Budget available
- Purpose for the need
- Attitude about life insurance policies
- Issues involved finding the best short-term price versus considerations of lowest long-term cost
- Age
- General health
- Tax advantages
- Liquidity at death
- Family Benefits

We recommend taking the following approach to life insurance; first, determine if there is a need for the insurance by identifying any financial loss that would occur in the event of your death. Examples of "financial loss" can include replacing the income of the family's wage earner(s), replacing the value of services provided to the family by a spouse not working outside the home, paying off a mortgage, paying final expenses, or providing for college funds to name a few. The next step is to determine your desires. For example, in addition to providing for your family's survivor income needs, you may also wish to address estate planning concerns, retirement, charitable bequests, or leave a legacy for your family. Because of the complexity involved in these decisions, thorough discussion with your financial advisor is recommended.

Life Insurance Basics

Life insurance is an agreement between you, the insured and an insurer. Under the terms of a life insurance policy, the insurer promises to pay a certain sum to a person you choose (your beneficiary) upon your death, in exchange for your premium payments. Proper life insurance coverage should provide you with peace of mind, since you know that those you care about will be financially protected after you die.

<u>There are many uses for life insurance.</u>

One of the most common reasons for buying life insurance is to replace the loss of income that would occur in the event of your death. When you die and your paychecks stop, your family may be left with limited resources. Proceeds from a life insurance policy make cash available to support your family almost immediately upon your death. Life insurance is also commonly used to pay any debts that you may leave behind. Life insurance can be used to pay off mortgages, car loans, and credit card debts, leaving other remaining assets intact for your family. Life insurance proceeds can also be used to pay for final expenses and estate taxes. Finally, life insurance can create an estate for your heirs.

<u>How much life insurance do you need?</u>

Your life insurance needs will depend on a number of factors, including whether you're married, the size of your family, the nature of your financial obligations, your career stage, and your goals. For example, when you're young, you may not have great need for life insurance. However, as you take on more responsibilities and your family grows, your need for life insurance increases.

There are plenty of tools to help you determine how much coverage you should have. Your best resource may be a financial professional. At the most basic level, the amount of life insurance coverage that you need corresponds directly to your answers to these questions:

- What immediate financial expenses e.g. debt repayment, funeral expenses would your family face upon your death?
- How much of your salary is devoted to current expenses and future needs?
- How long would your dependents need support if you were to die tomorrow?
- How much money would you want to leave for special situations upon your death, such as funding your children's education, gifts to charities, or an inheritance for your children?

Since your needs will change over time, you'll need to continually re-evaluate for appropriate levels of coverage.

How much life insurance can you afford?

How do you balance the cost of insurance coverage with the amount of coverage that your family needs? Just as several variables determine the amount of coverage that you need, many factors determine the cost of coverage. The type of policy that you choose, the amount of coverage, your age, and your health all play a part. The amount of coverage you can afford is tied to your current and expected future financial situation as well. A financial professional or insurance agent can be invaluable in helping you select the right insurance plan.

Proper life insurance coverage should provide you with peace of mind, since you know that those you care about will be financially protected after you die.

What's in a life insurance contract?

A life insurance contract is made up of legal provisions, your application (which identifies who you are and your medical declarations), and a policy specifications page that describes the policy you have selected, including any options and riders that you have purchased in return for an additional premium.

Provisions describe the conditions, rights, and obligations of the parties to the contract e.g., the grace period for payment of premiums, suicide and incontestability clauses.

The policy specifications page describes the amount to be paid upon your death and the amount of premiums required to keep the policy in effect. Also stated are any riders and options added to the standard policy. Some riders include the waiver of premium rider, which allows you to skip premium payments during periods of disability, the guaranteed insurability rider, which permits you to raise the amount of your insurance without a further medical exam, and accidental death benefits. The insurer may add an endorsement to the policy at the time of issue to amend a provision of the standard contract.

Types of life insurance policies

The two basic types of life insurance are term life and permanent (cash value) life.

Term policies provide life insurance protection for a specific period of time (subject to the claims-paying ability of the insurer). If you die during the coverage period, your beneficiary receives the policy death benefit. If you live to the end of the term, the policy simply terminates, unless it automatically renews for a new period. Term policies are available for periods of 1 to 30 years or more and may, in some cases, be renewed until you reach the age 95. Premium payments may increase, as with annually renewable 1-year (period) term, or level (equal) for up to 30-year term periods. Term policies offer the advantage of a level premium for the specified term. Some also offer options to continue coverage at the end of the term, or other special features

Permanent insurance policies provide protection for your entire life provided you pay the premium to keep the policy in force and subject to the claims-paying ability of the insurer. Premium payments are greater than necessary to provide the life insurance benefit in the early years of the policy, so that a reserve can be accumulated to make up the shortfall in premiums necessary to provide the insurance in the later years. Should the policy owner discontinue the policy, this reserve, known as the cash value, is returned to the policy owner, subject to applicable surrender or early withdrawal chargers.

Cash Value Life Insurance

Overview

Permanent insurance such as whole life, variable life, and universal life provides a death benefit, but will remain in effect as long as the premiums continue to be paid, regardless of how long the insured lives. Permanent insurance is accomplished by "over funding" the cost for the death benefit in the early years of the policy. This way the premium can remain level even as the insured ages and the cost of the life insurance increases. The "over funding" is accounted for in what is known as the cash value account. The cash value is the non-forfeiture value the policy owner is entitled to if all or part of the policy is terminated prior to payment of the death benefit. The cash value of the policy is often referred to as the investment component.

A major benefit of cash value insurance is that the policy owner can borrow from the insurance company against the accumulated cash value, often at a relatively low interest rate. Those funds can be used to finance retirement plans, pay college tuition, assist a child with a mortgage, or for any other purpose.

Permanent life insurance can be further broken down into the following basic categories:

Whole life:

You make level (equal) premium payments for life. The death benefit and minimum cash value are predetermined and guaranteed. Any guarantees associated with payment of death benefits, income options, or rates of return are based on the claims-paying ability of the insurer. Whole life insurance offers the predictability of level premium payments and can provide coverage for your entire life (instead of a set term). Whole life policies also have a cash value that you may be able to access under certain circumstances. For those who elect to buy a whole life policy, insurers will deposit the portion of the premium you pay that is not used for expenses, taxes, and mortality costs, in their general account. Insurers invest money in their general account primarily in long-term fixed-rate securities e.g., bonds, mortgages that typically provide modest returns to the company.

Some of the investment returns may be paid to the policy owner through dividend distributions (if applicable), but these returns reflect the insurance company's overall performance and are not guaranteed. Policy owners have no control over how the funds are invested or how the returns are generated. However, the insurance company will guarantee a minimum cash value accumulation.

> Caution: Guarantees are subject to the claims-paying ability of the issuing insurance company.

Whole life policies have several drawbacks. Because the cash value grows from primarily fixed-rate investments, they generally provide long-term returns that can be significantly less than what can be earned on other types of investments. Further, the policyowner is unable to influence the cash value account investment allocation.

In addition to whole life, insurers have developed other types of cash value policies, including variable life, universal life, and variable universal life, that offer more flexibility.

Universal life:

You may pay premiums at any time, in any amount (subject to certain limits), as long as policy expenses and the cost of insurance coverage are met. The amount of insurance can be changed, and the cash value will grow at a declared interest rate, which may vary over time. Universal life (UL) insurance can provide coverage for your entire lifetime. It also offers you the flexibility to pay your premiums at any time and in any amount (subject to some limits), as long as the policy expenses and cost of coverage are met. UL policies also have a cash value which can accumulate at a declared interest rate, and which you may be able to access under certain circumstances. With a universal life policy, the insurer invests the cash value in a fixed-rate account that is subject to change at regular intervals. Policy owners have no control over how the funds are invested. These accounts can yield attractive returns when rates on fixed-rate investments are high. However, long-term returns can't easily be predicted. The insurance company will provide a predetermined minimum interest rate on the cash value account. Universal life policies typically allow policy owners to raise or lower their premiums on an annual basis, unlike whole life or variable life. This flexibility with premium payments is one of the primary advantages of universal life.

Equity Indexed Universal Life:

Fixed indexed universal life works the same way as a UL policy, but with the addition of potential indexed interest. Indexed interest is credited based on changes in an external index or indexes, which you choose when you buy the policy. Your policy's cash value can grow tax-deferred, and you can access this value through loans and/or withdrawals. We have a separate section dedicated to this type of insurance coming up shortly.

Variable life:

As with whole life, you pay a level premium for life. However, the death benefit and cash value fluctuate depending on the performance of investments in what are known as subaccounts. A subaccount is a pool of investor funds professionally managed to pursue a stated investment objective. The policy owner selects the subaccounts in which the cash value should be invested. With a variable life insurance policy, policyholders have a choice in deciding how to invest the cash value account in their policy. The cash values are held in subaccounts. The insurance company will usually offer a wide variety of investment options, such as domestic investment vehicles and international stock, as well as a fixed rate option, so that the policy owner can diversify the cash value account with selections that are most appropriate for his or her personal financial situation. The return on the cash value account will be dependent on the performance of the underlying subaccounts. There is no guaranteed minimum cash value as with whole life. A variable policy may be appropriate for those who can tolerate the degree of risk associated with each type of investment and who want more control over their financial assets.

Variable Universal Life:

VUL is a combination of universal and variable life. You may pay premiums at any time, in any amount (subject to limits), as long as policy expenses and the cost of insurance coverage are met. The amount of insurance coverage can be changed, and the cash value goes up or down based on the performance of investments in the subaccounts. Also works the same as a UL policy but is invested into a portfolio of your choosing subject to the volatility of market conditions. Your policy's cash value can grow tax-deferred, and you can access this value through loans and/or withdrawals. Variable universal life insurance policies, a combination of universal life and variable life, provide policyholders with the investment option and control features of variable life and the premium and withdrawal features of universal life. Like variable life, variable universal life gives the policy owner the freedom to choose how his or her cash values are invested. A variable universal life policy may be appropriate for someone who can tolerate the higher degree of risk involved, and who wants maximum flexibility for premium payments and withdrawals.

> Caution: Variable life insurance and variable universal life insurance policies are offered by prospectus, which you can obtain from your financial professional or the insurance company. The prospectus contains detailed information about investment objectives, risks, charges, and expenses. You should read the prospectus and consider this information carefully before purchasing a variable life or variable universal life insurance policy.

Your beneficiaries

You must name a primary beneficiary to receive the proceeds of your insurance policy. You may name a contingent beneficiary to receive the proceeds if your primary beneficiary dies before the insured. Your beneficiary may be a person, corporation or other legal entity. You may name multiple beneficiaries and specify what percentage of the net death benefit each is to receive. You should carefully consider the ramifications of your beneficiary designations to ensure that your wishes are carried out as you intend.

Generally, you can change your beneficiary at any time. Changing your beneficiary usually requires nothing more than signing a new designation form and sending it to your insurance company. If you have named someone as an irrevocable (permanent) beneficiary, however, you will need that person's permission to adjust any of the policy's provisions.

Where can you buy life insurance?

You can often get insurance coverage from your employer (i.e., through a group life insurance plan) or through an association to which you belong (which may also offer group insurance). You can also buy insurance through a licensed life insurance agent or broker, or directly from an insurance company.

Any policy that you buy is only as good as the company that issues it, so investigate the company offering you the insurance. Ratings services such as A.M. Best, Moody's, and Standard & Poor's, evaluate an insurer's financial strength. The company offering you coverage should provide you with this information.

Note: Variable life and Variable Universal Life insurance policies are offered by prospectus, which you can obtain from your financial professional or the insurance company. The prospectus contains detailed information about investment objects, risks, charges, and expenses. You should read the prospectus and consider this information carefully before purchasing variable life or variable universal life insurance policy.

An Illustration as to How Traditional Permanent Insurance Works

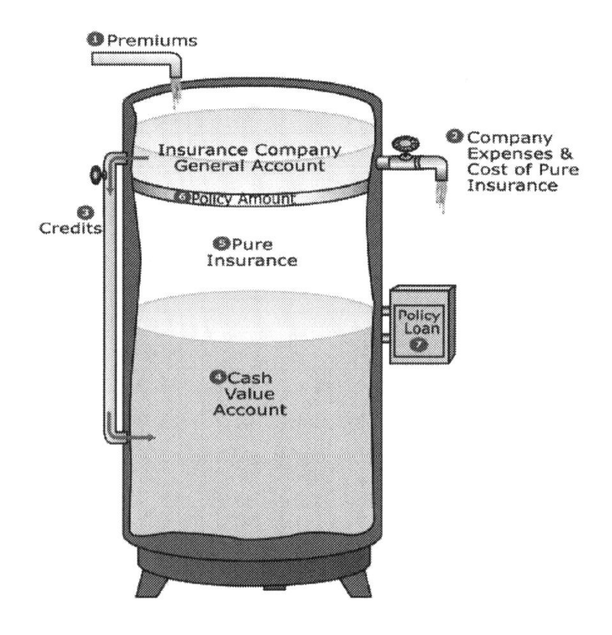

1. The premium you "pour in" is fixed for the life of the policy. As you age, the cost of insuring your life increases. However, your premium stays the same, because the company projects this expense in advance and factors it into the premium at the onset.
2. As you pay your premium, the insurance company deducts all of its expenses, premium taxes, and the cost of pure insurance (net amount of risk coverage), or mortality cost.
3. The remainder of your premium represents a portion of the insurance company's investment portfolio. Your cash value account is credited with a fixed amount (predetermined by your contract) at the end of each premium period.
4. Like water in a tank, the level of your cash value rises over time.
5. As the cash value increases, the amount of risk coverage (or pure insurance) in the policy decreases.
6. When you die, your beneficiary receives the "full tank" of the policy amount, which is the sum of the cash value and the pure insurance.
7. You may take a policy loan in an amount not to exceed the policy's cash surrender value less the annual loan interest. Repayment replenishes your cash value; any loan balance outstanding (plus interest due) at the time from your death would be deducted from the policy amount.

However, life insurance is not "one size fits all".

Like other strategies mentioned in this book, there is rarely, if ever, one way to accomplish an objective. This is also true with life insurance. As you can see, there are many types and purposes for life insurance. Our goal with this chapter is to introduce you to the types briefly, while also providing additional ideas which generally do not make their way into financial books on the street.

The "living benefits" of your policy

Loans

One of the benefits of cash value life insurance is the ability to borrow from the insurer using the policy cash value as collateral. All permanent life policies typically allow policyholders to borrow against their cash value.

The insurer makes the loan from the insurance company's general funds, using the policy's cash value as collateral. Some policies set the interest rate at an amount equal to the amount the company credits to the policy's cash value. Other policies set the amount slightly higher than the amount credited to the cash value. Interest starts accruing immediately, and is either fixed for the life of the contract or changes periodically in step with a published bond index.

> Caution: Taking a loan against an insurance policy reduces both the cash value and the death benefit. While there is no requirement to pay back a loan, if it is not repaid before the insured's death, any outstanding loans and interest will reduce the death benefit that beneficiaries receive.

> Caution: Policy loans generally do not generate immediate tax liability for the policyowner as long as the policy remains in force. However, if the policy lapses or is surrendered, the policyowner will be required to include the outstanding loan balance as gross income to the extent the loan proceeds exceed the investment (premiums) in the policy.

Withdrawals

Variable universal life and universal life insurance policies also allow policyholders to make withdrawals. To make a withdrawal, one only needs to pay a small administrative fee. The downside to policy withdrawals is that they permanently reduce the policy's cash value and death benefit. In addition, if the policy is classified as a modified endowment contract (MEC), withdrawals, including loans and partial surrenders, will be subject to immediate taxation to the extent that the policy's cash value exceeds the premiums paid. In addition, withdrawals from a MEC made prior to age 59½ may result in a 10 percent penalty, unless an exception applies.

21

Equity Indexed Universal Life

There is one other type of Permanent Life Insurance, Equity Indexed Universal Life, which is unique enough to merit discussion independently of the other types of insurance in the previous chapter.

What is EIUL?

Equity-indexed universal life insurance (EIUL) is a form of universal life insurance, meaning it is permanent, cash value insurance. Like universal life insurance, EIUL offers you the ability to change your level of protection, premium amounts, and payment frequency. Both universal life (UL) and EIUL pay interest on excess premium contributions, creating a cash value. Traditional UL and EIUL both pay a minimum guaranteed interest rate on cash accumulations.

However, EIUL differs from traditional UL regarding how excess interest is determined. Typical UL insurance provides a guaranteed minimum interest rate, plus an excess interest rate when the insurance company's investments perform well. EIUL policies are different. Most EIUL policies have two separate accounts that can be used to credit interest. One account has a fixed interest rate that is declared by the insurance issuer periodically. The second account provides an equity index option that offers you the opportunity to earn rates of interest based on positive equity (stock) market returns. However, the cash value of the EIUL policy is not exposed to losses due to negative market returns.

Caution: Guarantees are subject to the claims-paying ability of the life insurance issuer.

How Does EIUL Work?

Combines aspects of universal and variable life insurance

EIUL combines aspects of both universal and variable life insurance. EIUL is universal life insurance since it has an interest crediting rate, and excess cash values are not exposed to the equity market as is the case with variable life insurance. However, EIUL is similar to variable life insurance because cash accumulations are based on equity market performance. Cash accumulations of variable life insurance policies are determined by the performance of the subaccounts in which your money is invested and will rise if your investments do well, or fall if your investments do poorly. Cash accumulations of EIUL policies are determined by the performance of a stock market index. However, unlike variable life, EIUL cash accumulations are not invested in subaccounts, so they are not subject to risk of loss due to poor market returns. Instead, EIUL cash accumulations earn interest based on the gains, if any, in the stock market index. Interest is credited to cash accumulations within an EIUL policy in much the same way as interest is earned in an equity-indexed annuity.

There are a number of facets in an EIUL policy which differ from traditional universal life and variable life insurance. Most of these items relate to how the interest is credited to the cash value of the EIUL policy.

> Caution: Variable life insurance and variable universal life insurance policies are offered by prospectus, which you can obtain from your financial professional or the insurance company. The prospectus contains detailed information about investment objectives, risks, charges, and expenses. You should read the prospectus and consider this information carefully before purchasing a variable life or variable universal life insurance policy.

The equity index

The amount of interest credited to your cash value is tied to the performance of your policy's particular equity index, so that in years where the index performs well, the interest credited to your cash value rises, whereas in years where the index performs poorly, your interest rate falls. Most EIUL policies guarantee that your interest rate will never fall below zero so that you won't lose money if the stock market index declines. EIUL policies commonly have a limit or cap on the amount of interest that is credited to your cash value. The cap on your interest earnings is applied, in part, to offset the issuer's assumption of any negative returns that may occur in the stock market index.

Issuers use different equity indexes, such as the Dow Jones Industrial Average, Lehman Brothers Bond Index, and NASDAQ, but the most common index applied is the S&P 500.

Participation rate and cap

The participation rate determines how much of the index's gain will be used to calculate the interest rate that is applied to your cash value. Some EIUL issuers guarantee a 100 percent participation rate for the duration of the policy, while other issuers reserve the right to change the participation rate at their discretion. If the participation rate is 100 percent, then all of the gain in the equity index will be credited as interest to your cash value, subject to a cap. The cap is the maximum percentage of interest that will be applied to your cash value during any indexing period. The participation rate and cap applied by the EIUL issuer often depends, at least in part, on the type of indexing method used.

> Example(s): If the equity index used in the EIUL policy gained 12 percent during the index period, and the participation rate is 90 percent, then the percentage of interest credited to your cash value is 10.8 percent (12 x.90). Furthering the example, if a cap of nine percent also applies, then the percentage interest credited to your cash value would be nine percent, not 10.8.

EIUL Features Similar to Traditional Universal Life Insurance

Permanent (cash value) life insurance

Both EIUL and UL are permanent (cash value) insurance. Each type of insurance usually credits your cash value with a guaranteed minimum interest rate plus an excess interest rate. EIUL and UL also offer you flexibility through the ability to change your level of protection, premium amounts, and payment frequency. In this way, your policy can keep pace with changes in your life and your corresponding insurance needs. The policies' cash values can be accessed by you during your lifetime. Cash values of each type of policy grow tax deferred.

> Caution: Guarantees are subject to the claims-paying ability of the life insurance issuer.

You can change your premium payments

Generally, each policy allows you to increase, decrease, and even skip premiums after the first policy year, as long as the cash value is large enough to cover policy expense charges. You have the ability to change the amount or frequency of your premium payment without giving the insurer prior notice. Most EIUL and UL issuers suggest a target premium amount to keep the policy in force.

> Caution: If your cash value isn't sufficient to cover the current expense and mortality charges, you may be required to make an additional premium payment in order to prevent a policy lapse.

Policy loans

As cash value life insurance, both EIUL and UL insurance allow you to borrow from cash surrender values using a policy loan. Policy loans are allowed under the terms of your insurance contract. Loan interest is charged on any amount of cash value borrowed that is not considered a withdrawal. The interest rate on a policy loan is declared by the policy issuer in advance.

> Caution: If you die with an outstanding policy loan against your account, your death benefit is reduced by the amount of the outstanding loan balance.

Guaranteed death benefit

Like most UL insurance, some EIUL policies offer a guaranteed death benefit. The insurance company guarantees that as long as a minimum premium is paid on time the coverage will not lapse. The minimum death benefit guarantee may last the first five policy years or longer. If the lifetime death benefit guarantee option is selected, the coverage can never be terminated by the insurance company as long as the policy premium is paid when due, regardless of equity-indexed or UL interest performance. Usually there is an additional cost for the lifetime guarantee which reduces your policy's cash value growth potential.

EIUL Disadvantages

One disadvantage of equity-indexed universal life insurance is the potential for little or no gain in cash values during periods of negative stock market returns compared to minimum interest guarantees of universal life insurance. Also, the interest rate cap limits the upside potential compared to the unlimited growth potential of variable life insurance. EIUL has more "moving parts" than either universal or variable life such as caps, participation rates, and crediting methods which can be confusing. Also, policy surrender charges decrease your cash values if you decide to surrender the policy prior to the end of the surrender period.

Another disadvantage of UL also applies to EIUL. The cost of insurance, along with other fees and charges, reduces your policy's cash value. In addition, the cost of insurance will increase each year as your (the insured) age increases. If you choose to reduce or skip premiums, it is possible that your cash value may not be sufficient to cover the cost of insurance increases over time.

When you take a policy loan, the loan proceeds you receive come from the general fund of the insurance company. The loan amount is not actually withdrawn from your cash value account. However, an amount of your cash value equal to the loan amount is marked as collateral for the loan. The collateral amount usually is credited with a lower interest rate than the remaining cash value. The reduced interest credited to a portion of your cash value will slow the growth of your cash value. Also, unpaid loans will reduce the death benefit payable to your survivors.

In summary, here is a list detailing the benefits of ***Permanent Cash Value Life Insurance*** which is a very unique and flexible financial planning tool to help you and your family achieve real financial independence. Properly structured and properly funded Cash Value Life Insurance provides you with these exceptional benefits:

- The first and foremost benefit of Cash Value Life Insurance is that it provides your family with the money they need in the event of your death: to replace your lost income, pay-off mortgages and pay-off consumer debts, along with paying any medical expenses and burial expenses as a result of your passing.
- By purchasing cash value life insurance while you are young the premiums are low, and will remain level throughout your entire life, if properly funded.
- You own the policy instead of renting it. You have complete control.
- You don't have to re-qualify for the death protection as you grow older.
- Cash Value Life Insurance is a forced savings plan. It forces you to *Pay Yourself First!* When you understand that a portion of all you earn is yours to keep but not to spend, great wealth won't be far behind.
- Unlike qualified plans, there are no caps (limits) on how much money you can save each year. You are only limited by the size of the policy.
- Your cash values accumulate on a tax deferred basis.
- You have a liquid emergency fund for life's unexpected events.
- As the cash values accumulate, you are buying and paying for less death benefit.
- The cash values can be accessed income tax-free and penalty free prior to age 59 ½, as opposed to the early withdrawal penalty in other plans.
- Because of the disability waiver of premiums and death benefits, C.V. life insurance is the only self-completing savings, college funding and supplemental retirement plan!
- Cash value life insurance is generally not attachable by creditors. Check your state statue.
- Cash value life insurance doesn't count as an asset when you apply for college financial aid.
- By over-funding a cash value life insurance policy, up to the MEC guidelines, it can become investment grade life insurance.
- The cash accumulated in your policy can provide you with a tax-free income in retirement. You can take withdrawals up to the cost basis and then borrow the remainder.

- You'll have the protection of life insurance in your retirement years, to replace lost pension and Social Security income at your death.
- Unlike qualified plans and annuities, the death benefits and cash values are transferred income tax free to your beneficiaries.
- Cash value life insurance generally bypasses probate and the settlement is private, with no public records.
- Cash value life insurance can be used to pay income taxes on qualified plans, annuities and estate taxes at your death.
- Safety—All 50 states have something similar to FDIC for life insurance policies and annuities . . . plus, insurance companies must, by law, cover at least 100% of their liabilities with reserves, hence the term *100% legal reserve life insurance company.* There are also regulations as to the percentage that can be held in certain forms of assets. This system has produced a remarkable overall record of solvency and safety.
- Guarantees—Only Life Insurance and Annuities guarantee your investment principal and offer you minimum growth guarantees for the life of the contract.

As you can see, permanent Cash Value Life Insurance, besides providing protection for your family, is an extraordinary savings tool. It enjoys unique income tax treatment, safety, guarantees, privacy and self-completion features, making it an extremely valuable addition to almost everyone's portfolio and financial plan.

22

Other Insurance Coverage

In addition to the some of the risks we've already talked about, there are myriad others to consider as well. This chapter deals with three main segments.

1. **Umbrella Liability Insurance**

When your local weather forecaster tells you that it's going to rain, what do you do? That's easy—you reach for your umbrella. So why not purchase an umbrella that can protect you in stormy financial weather? Umbrella liability insurance (ULI) can do just that. By providing liability protection above and beyond the basic coverage that homeowners/renters and auto insurance policies offer, ULI can protect you against the catastrophic losses that can occur if you are sued.

1. Some common real-life examples include:
   (a) A doctor's car backs up into an unseen pedestrian, causing bodily harm or property damage.
   (b) A gathering is hosted at a doctor's home with alcoholic beverages served. A guest is over-served and is involved in an auto accident.
   (c) A child attending a birthday party trips and falls on the doctor's property.

Although ULI can be purchased as a separate policy, your insurer will require that you have basic liability coverage i.e., homeowners/renters insurance, auto insurance, or both before you can purchase an umbrella liability policy. ULI is often referred to as excess coverage. If you are found to be legally responsible for injuring someone or damaging someone's property, the umbrella policy will either pay for the part of the claim in excess of the limits of your basic liability policy, or pay for certain losses that are not covered.

Why now? It's not even raining!

These days, it's not unusual to hear of $2 million, $10 million, and even $20 million court judgments against individuals. If someone is injured in your home, or if you cause a serious auto accident, you could have to pay such a judgment. If you don't have an umbrella liability policy at the time of the accident, anything above the limits of your homeowners/renters or auto insurance policy will have to come out of your pocket.

Here's an example of how ULI works to protect you. Say you have an auto insurance policy with a liability limit of $100,000 per accident. You also have a $1 million umbrella liability policy. You're later found responsible for a serious automobile accident, and the court finds you liable for $700,000 in damages. In this case, your auto insurance would pay the first $100,000 of the judgment, which would satisfy the deductible under your umbrella policy. Your umbrella policy would then cover the portion of the judgment not covered by your auto insurance ($600,000).

You should also be aware that certain types of liability claims e.g., libel and slander are not covered under basic homeowners, auto, or other types of insurance policies. An endorsement can be added to these policies to provide some protection against these types of personal injury claims. Or, you can purchase ULI, which does cover these claims.

What's covered?

A typical umbrella liability policy provides the following protection, up to the coverage limits specified in the policy:

- Protection for claims of bodily injuries or property damage caused by you, members of your household, or hazards on your property, for which you are found legally liable;
- Personal liability coverage for incidents that occur on or off your property;
- Additional protection above your basic auto policy for auto-related liabilities;

- Protection against non-business-related personal injury claims, such as slander, libel, wrongful eviction, and false arrest;
- Legal defense costs for a covered loss, including lawyers' fees and associated court costs.

What's not covered?

Umbrella liability insurance typically provides extremely broad coverage. Furthermore, if something is not expressly excluded from coverage, it is covered. Exclusions vary from one insurer to another and from one policy to another, but the following are some items typically excluded from coverage:

- Intentional damage caused by you or a member of your family or household;
- Damages arising out of business or professional pursuits;
- Liability that you accept under the terms of a contract or agreement;
- Liability related to the ownership, maintenance, and use of aircraft, nontraditional watercraft e.g., jet skis, air boats, and most recreational vehicles;
- Damage to property owned, used, or maintained by you, the insured;
- Damage covered under a workmen's compensation policy;
- Liability arising as a result of war or insurrection.

How big of an umbrella are we talking about?

Determining how much liability coverage you need is not an exact science. You might think that you need only enough liability insurance to protect your assets, but a large judgment against you could easily wipe out your assets and put your future earnings in jeopardy. That's why you should also consider factors such as how often you have guests in your home, whether you operate a home-based business, how much you drive, whether you have teenage drivers in your home, and whether your lifestyle gives the impression that you have "deep pockets."

Coverage limits vary, but a typical policy will provide liability coverage worth $1 million to $10 million. Of course, as your coverage limit increases, the premium will also increase. You need to decide both how much insurance you need and how much insurance you can afford. You'll want to have enough protection, but not too much. Look at it this way; have you ever seen a five-year-old child walking under a big golf umbrella or a 300 lb. football player using a pocket-sized umbrella? One has too much protection and the other not enough. Your insurance agent can help you determine how much coverage you need.

Where can I buy an umbrella liability policy?

Almost any insurer who writes auto and home insurance policies will also sell umbrella liability policies. In fact, you may be eligible for a multi-policy discount if you purchase an umbrella policy from your current insurer. Of course, it's important to shop around and make sure that you're getting the right coverage for your needs and the most coverage for your money. If you want to do some research on your own, try surfing the Internet, where you can get price quotes and answers to your questions in an instant.

Personal Umbrella Liability Policy

A personal umbrella liability policy is a broad form of liability coverage that protects you against large losses, or losses not covered by basic personal liability insurance. Issued with higher liability limits than basic liability coverage (a $1 million limit is common), an umbrella policy can be purchased as a stand-alone policy. More commonly, however, it is added using a rider to an existing homeowners or automobile insurance policy. If the insured is found legally responsible for injuring someone or for damaging property, then the umbrella policy will pay either that part of the claim in excess of the liability limits of the insured's basic liability coverage or for certain losses not covered by basic personal liability insurance, including personal injury and unusual occurrences, up to the limits of the umbrella liability policy.

2. Long Term Care Insurance

Although this likely isn't a concern for younger clients, as our clients age this definitely becomes relevant to the planning process. Protecting against long-term debilitations requiring care can quickly drain a client's wealth.

An insurance policy paying some or all the costs associated with in-home health care or nursing home for those unable to perform the basic activities of daily living. 65% of individuals over the age of 65 will require at least some type of long-term care service during their lifetime (according to Centers for Medicare & Medicaid Services).

Is your retirement protected?

These days we have many things about which we should be concerned: the economy, the market, our portfolio, etc. To us, it seems every day is filled with more bad news. It is important to also consider two very important things as you approach retirement: the amount of income you will need to maintain your standard of living and the amount of expenses you can expect to have. You must include long term care expenses in your planning process! An article by the *Motley Fool* in July 2007 stated the biggest danger to any plan for retirement is failing to consider the impact of health-care costs.

You are likely aware that as you age you will probably need some form of care. Typically, people underestimate how a long term illness can and will affect their retirement income, their nest egg, and their relationships. Generally, men expect their spouse to take care of them when their health changes. Women tend to be more realistic since they know they will probably live longer and also realize that their own health will change dramatically as they age. 95% of residents in nursing homes are elderly women.

Have you determined what percentage of your assets is set aside toward the cost of paying for long term care? In most cases, wealth preservation is a major goal for most retirees and enduring a long term care loss in addition to taxes and market loss is simply too much to bear. Because most individuals do not save/invest enough to pay for long term care, it is in your best interest to evaluate a long term care proposal. There is no specific plan for every situation and there are many options available, so be sure to design a plan which fits your specific situation.

Some statistics for you to consider: for every 1000 Americans over the age of 65:

1. Five will suffer a catastrophic loss of their home due to fire.

2. Seventy will have an automobile accident serious enough to warrant filing an insurance claim.
3. Six hundred will need some form of long term care.

There are numerous studies indicating a significant relationship between declining health and declining wealth. With this in mind, would it make sense to evaluate options to provide peace of mind by reviewing long term care coverage?

The reality is most people are unable to afford long term care expenses without financial assistance. Additionally, it's virtually impossible to place a price tag on caregivers' lives. This decision is more than just money. It's about relationships within your family and how those are impacted when/if you require care.

You might be thinking, "I have health insurance, Medicare, Medicaid, etc." Let's review these options in greater detail.

1. ***Health Insurance:*** Custodial care is not included in any medical plan. The majority of care for the elderly who need long term care is custodial.
2. ***Medicare:*** Medicare is not intended to pay for long term care. Even the Social Security Administration, at the urging of Congress, has added wording to their annual statements sent to Americans that long term care expenses are outside the scope of the Medicare program.
3. ***Medicaid:*** The Deficit Reduction Act of 2005 severely impacted the viability of Medicaid to be a long term care planning tool. Regardless of how you feel about the practice of artificial impoverishment to qualify for Medicaid benefits, the government is taking concrete steps to return the Medicaid program to its original intended mission; as a safety net for the poor.

Long term care insurance is a solid defensive strategy for your portfolio in that owning such a policy would prevent spending portfolio assets. It provides a reliable source of tax-efficient liquidity that is separate but integrated to your overall financial plan. It is financially sensible to spend a minimal amount every month in premiums versus hundreds of thousands in potential care costs. Without long term care insurance, your retirement asset could ultimately be ravaged and your relationships strained.

No one likes to anticipate getting old and needing care, but it is a reality we all have to face. The solutions for coverage are much better these days than in the past. Do yourself a favor and evaluate what coverage is appropriate for you. Your family will thank you.

3. Auto/Home Insurance

Scheduling a meeting with your P & C (Property & Casualty) Agent to determine the appropriate coverage limits is critical to protect your home, vehicle, and personal items.

Let us offer a word about deductibles. As your wealth grows, consider raising your deductibles to save money on your monthly premium while self-insuring the deductible amount.

IV

Distribute Your Wealth

23

Retirement Income: The Transition into Retirement

As you shift towards retirement there are many variables to evaluate. The purpose of this chapter is to provide you a framework including financial and emotional considerations.

When it comes to transitioning into retirement, timing really is everything. The age at which you retire can have an enormous impact on your overall retirement income situation, so you'll want to make sure you've considered your decision from every angle. In fact, you may find that deciding when to retire is actually the product of a series of smaller decisions and calculations.

1) *How long should you plan for your retirement?* The good news is that, statistically, you're going to live for a long time. That's also the bad news, though; because that means your retirement income plan is going to have to be sufficient to provide for your needs over (potentially) a long period of time. How long? The average 65-year-old American can expect to live for over 18.6 additional years (Source: National Vital Statistics Reports, Volume 58, Number 1, August 2009). Keep in mind as well that life expectancy has increased at a steady pace over the years, and is expected to continue increasing. The bottom line is that it's not unreasonable to plan for a retirement period that lasts for 30 years or more.
2) *Can you afford the retirement you want?* Separate from the issue of whether you're emotionally ready to retire is the question of whether you're financially ready. Simply, can you afford to do everything you want in retirement? Of course, the answer to

this question is anything but simple. It depends on your goals in retirement i.e. how much the lifestyle you want will cost, the amount of income you can count on, and your personal savings. It also depends on how long a retirement you want to plan for and what your assumptions are regarding future inflation and earnings.

3) *Are you thinking of retiring early?* Retiring early can be wonderful if you're ready both emotionally and financially. Consider the financial aspect of an early retirement with great care, though. An early retirement can dramatically change your retirement finances because it affects your income plan in two major ways. First, you're giving up what could be prime earning years, a period of time during which you could be adding to your retirement savings. More importantly, though, you're increasing the number of years that your retirement savings will need to provide for your expenses, and a few years can make a tremendous difference. There are other factors to consider as well:

    - A longer retirement period means a greater potential for inflation to eat away at your purchasing power.
    - You can begin receiving Social Security retirement benefits as early as age 62. However, your benefit may be as much as 20% to 30% less than if you waited until full retirement (age 65 to 67, depending on the year you were born).
    - If you're covered by an employer pension plan, check to make sure it won't be negatively affected by your early retirement. Because the greatest accrual of benefits generally occurs during your final years of employment, it's possible that early retirement could effectively reduce the benefits you receive.
    - If you plan to start using your 401(k) or traditional IRA savings before you turn 59½, you may have to pay a 10% early distribution penalty tax in addition to any regular income tax due (with some exceptions, including payments made from a 401(k) plan due to your separation from service in or after the year you turn 55, and distributions due to disability).
    - You're not eligible for Medicare until you turn 65. Unless you'll be eligible for retiree health benefits through your employer (or have coverage through your spouse's plan),

or you take another job that offers health insurance, you'll need to calculate the cost of paying for insurance or health care out-of-pocket, at least until you can receive Medicare coverage.

4) *Are you thinking of postponing retirement?* Postponing retirement lets you continue to add to your retirement savings. That's especially advantageous if you're saving in tax-deferred accounts, and if you're receiving employer contributions. For example, if you retire at age 65 instead of age 55, and manage to save an additional $20,000 per year in your 401(k) at an 8% rate of return during that time, you can add an extra $312,909 to your retirement fund. (This is a hypothetical example and is not intended to reflect the actual performance of any specific investment.) Even if you're no longer adding to your retirement savings, delaying retirement postpones the date that you'll need to start withdrawing from your savings. That could significantly enhance your savings' potential to last throughout your lifetime.

Of course, there are other factors that you should consider.

- Postponing full retirement gives you additional transition time if you need it. If you're considering a new career or volunteer opportunities in retirement, you could lay the groundwork by taking classes or trying out your new role part-time.
- Postponing retirement may allow you to delay taking Social Security retirement benefits, potentially increasing your benefit.
- If you postpone retirement beyond age 70½, you'll need to begin taking requirement minimum distributions from any traditional IRAs and employer-sponsored retirement plans (other than your current employer's retirement plan), even if you do not need the funds.

5) *Do you plan to work in retirement?* An increasing number of employees nearing retirement plan to work for at least some period of time during their retirement years. The obvious advantage of working during retirement is that you'll be earning money and relying less on your retirement savings, leaving more to potentially grow for the future and helping your savings to last

longer. However, there are also non-economic reasons for working during retirement. Many retirees work for personal fulfillment, to stay mentally and physically active, to enjoy the social benefits of working, or to try their hand at something new. The reasons are as varied as the retirees themselves. If you're thinking of working during a portion of your retirement, you'll want to consider carefully how it might affect your overall retirement income plan. For example,

- If you continue to work, will you have access to affordable health care (more and more employers are offering this important benefit to part-time employees)?

- Will working in retirement allow you to delay receiving Social Security retirement benefits? If so, your annual benefit, when you begin receiving benefits, may be higher.

- If you'll be receiving Social Security benefits while working, how will your work income affect the amount of Social Security benefits that you receive? Additional earnings can increase benefits in future years. However, for years before you reach full retirement age, $1 in benefits will generally be withheld for every $2 you earn over the annual earnings limit ($14,160 in 2010). Special rules apply in the year that you reach full retirement age.

6) *How Much Annual Retirement Income Will You Need?* How much annual income will you need in retirement? If you aren't able to answer this question, you're not ready to make a decision about retiring. And, if it's been more than a year since you've thought about it, it's time to revisit your calculations. Your whole retirement income plan starts with your target annual income, and there are a significant number of factors to consider; start out with a poor estimate of your needs, and your plan is off-track before you've even begun.

These are general guidelines when thinking about retirement. It's common to discuss desired annual retirement income as a percentage of your current income. Depending on who you're talking to, that percentage could be anywhere from 60% to 90%, or even more, of your current income. The appeal of this approach lies in its simplicity, and the fact that there's a fairly common-sense analysis of underlying it. Your current income sustains your present lifestyle, so taking that income and reducing it by a specific percentage to reflect the fact that there will be certain expenses e.g., payroll taxes you'll no longer be liable for, will, theoretically, allow you to sustain your current lifestyle.

The problem with this approach is that it doesn't account for your specific situation. If you intend to travel extensively in retirement, for example, you might easily need 100% or more of your current income to get by. It is fine to use a percentage of your current income as a benchmark, but it's worth going through all of your current expenses in detail, and really thinking about how those expenses will change over time as you transition into retirement. Some questions to consider: What is the lifestyle that you envision? Do you expect to travel extensively? Take up or rediscover a hobby? Do you plan to take classes? Whatever your plan, try to assign a corresponding dollar cost.

Other specific considerations include:

- *Inflation*—Inflation is the risk that the purchasing power of a dollar will decline over time, due to the rising cost of goods and services. If inflation runs at its historical average of about 3%, a given sum of money will lose half its purchasing power in 23 years. Perspective: $50k now would be $90,306 in 20 years
- *Housing costs*—if your mortgage isn't already paid off, will it be paid soon? Do you plan to relocate to a less or more expensive area? Will you downsize?
- *Work-related expenses*—you're likely to eliminate some costs associated with your current job e.g. commuting, clothing, dry-cleaning, retirement savings contributions, in addition to payroll taxes.
- *Health care*—healthcare costs can have a significant impact on your retirement finances. This can be particularly true in the early years if you retire before you're eligible for Medicare.
- *Long-term care costs*—the potential costs involved in an extended nursing home stay can be catastrophic.

- *Entertainment*—it's not uncommon to see an increase in general entertainment expenses like dining out.
- *Children/parents*—are you responsible financially for family members? Could that change in future years?
- *Gifting*—do you plan on making gifts to family members or a favorite charity? Do you want to ensure that funds are left to your heirs at your death?

Traditionally, retirement income has been described as a "three-legged stool" comprised of Social Security, traditional employer pension income, and individual savings and investments. With fewer and fewer individuals covered by traditional employer pensions, though, the analogy doesn't really hold up well today.

1) *Social Security Retirement Income:*

*T*oday, 94% of U.S. workers are covered by Social Security (Source: SSA-Social Security Program Fact Sheet, 2009). The amount of Social Security retirement benefit that you're entitled to is based on the number of years you've been working and the amount you've earned. Your benefit is calculated using a formula that takes into account your 35 highest earning years.

The earliest that you can begin receiving Social Security retirement benefits is age 62. If you decide to start collecting benefits before your full retirement age (which ranges from 65 to 67, depending on the year you were born), there's a major drawback to consider: your monthly retirement benefit will be permanently reduced. In fact, if you begin collecting retirement benefits at age 62, each monthly benefit will be 20% to 30% less than it would be at full retirement age. The exact amount of the reduction will depend on the year you were born. Conversely, you can get a higher payout by delaying retirement past your full retirement age. The government increases your payout every month that you delay retirement, up to age 70.

If you begin receiving retirement benefits at age 62, however, even though your monthly benefit is less than it would be if you waited until normal retirement age, you'll end up receiving more benefit checks. For example, if your normal retirement age is 66, and you opt to receive Social

Security retirement benefits at age 62 rather than waiting until 66, you'll receive 48 additional monthly benefit payments.

The good news is that, for many people, Social Security will provide a monthly benefit each and every month of retirement, and the benefit will be periodically adjusted for inflation. The bad news is that, for many people, Social Security alone isn't going to provide enough income in retirement. For example, according to the quick calculator on Social Security's website, www.ssa.gov, an individual born in 1944 who currently earns $100,000 a year can expect to receive approximately $23,000 annually at full retirement age, which in this case would be age 66. Of course, your actual benefits will depend on your work history, earnings, and retirement age. The point is that Social Security will probably make up only a portion of your total retirement income needs.

2) *Traditional Employer Pensions*

If you're entitled to receive a traditional pension, you're lucky; fewer Americans are covered by them every year. If you haven't already selected a payout option, you'll want to carefully consider your choices. And, whether or not you've already chosen a payout option, you'll want to make sure you know exactly how much income your pension will provide, and whether or not it will adjust for inflation.

In a traditional pension plan also known as a defined benefit plan, your retirement benefit is generally an annuity, payable over your lifetime, beginning at the plan's normal retirement age, typically age 65. Many plans allow you to retire early; for example, at age 55 or earlier. However, if you choose early retirement, your pension benefit is actuarially reduced to account for the fact that payments are beginning earlier, and are payable for a longer period of time.

If you're married, the plan generally must pay your benefit as a qualified joint and survivor annuity (QJSA). A QJSA provides a monthly payment for as long as either you or your spouse is alive. The payments under a QJSA are generally smaller than under a single-life annuity because they continue until both you and your spouse have died.

Your spouse's QJSA survivor benefit is typically 50% of the amount you receive during your joint lives. However, depending on the terms of your employer's plan, you may be able to elect a spousal survivor benefit of up to 100% of the amount you receive during your joint lives. Generally, the greater the survivor benefit you choose, the smaller the amount you will receive during your joint lives. If your spouse consents in writing, you can decline the QJSA and elect a single-life annuity or another option offered by the plan.

The best option for you depends on your individual situation, including your (and your spouse's) age, health, and other financial resources. If you're at all unsure about your pension, including which options are available to you, talk to your financial professional familiar with pension maximization strategies. Often the best choice is not the one offered on the election form provided by your employer and unfortunately your selection is irrevocable.

3) *Personal Savings*

Most people are not going to be able to rely on Social Security retirement benefits to provide for all of their needs. Also, traditional pensions are becoming rarer. That leaves the last leg of the three-legged stool, or personal savings, to carry most of the burden when it comes to your retirement income plan.

Your personal savings are funds that you've accumulated in tax-advantaged retirement accounts like 401(k) plans, 403(b) plans, 457(b) plans, and IRAs, as well as any investments you hold outside of tax-advantaged accounts.

Until now, when it came to personal savings, your focus was probably on accumulation; building as large a nest egg as possible. As you transition into retirement, however, that focus changes. Rather than accumulation, you're going to need to look at your personal savings in terms of distribution and income potential. The bottom line is that you want to maximize the ability of your personal savings to provide annual income during your retirement years, closing the gap between your projected annual income needs and the funds you'll be receiving from Social Security and from any pension payout.

Some of the factors you'll need to consider, in the context of your overall plan, include:

- Your general asset allocation—the challenge is to provide, with reasonable certainty, for the annual income you will need, while balancing that need with other considerations such as liquidity, how long you need your funds to last, your risk tolerance, and anticipated rates of return.

- Specific investments and products—should you consider an annuity? Municipal bonds? CDs? TIPs?
- Your withdrawal rate—how much can you afford to withdraw each year without exhausting your portfolio? You'll need to take into account your asset allocation, projected returns, your distribution period, and whether you expect to use both principal and income, or income alone. You'll also need to consider how much fluctuation in income you can tolerate from month to month, and year to year.
- The order in which you tap various accounts—tax considerations can affect which accounts you should use first, and which you should defer using until later.
- Required minimum distributions (RMDs)—you'll want to consider up front how you'll deal with required withdrawals from tax-advantaged accounts like 401(k)s and traditional IRAs, or whether they'll be a factor at all. After age 70½, if you withdraw less than your RMD, you'll pay a penalty tax equal to 50% of the amount you failed to withdraw (elaborated on in pages 109-112).
- Working in retirement—part-time work, regular consulting, or a full second career can all provide you with a valuable income.
- Your home—if you have built up substantial home equity, you may be able to tap it as a source of retirement income. You could sell your home, then downsize or buy in a lower cost region, investing that freed-up cash to produce income or to be used as needed. Another possibility is borrowing against the value of your home (a course that should be explored with caution).
- Permanent life insurance—although not the primary function of life insurance, an existing permanent life insurance policy that has cash value can sometimes be a potential source of retirement income. (Policy loans and withdrawals can reduce the cash value, reduce or eliminate the death benefit, and can have negative tax consequences.)

A common question to ask is *What if you still don't have enough?* If there's no possibility that you're going to be able to afford the retirement you want, your options are limited:

1. Postpone retirement—you'll be able to continue to add to your retirement savings. More importantly, delaying retirement postpones the date that you'll need to start withdrawing from your personal savings. Depending on your individual circumstances, this can make an enormous difference in your overall retirement income plan.
2. Reevaluate retirement expectations—you might consider ratcheting down your goals and expectations in retirement to a level that better aligns with your financial means. That doesn't necessarily mean a dramatic lifestyle change—even small adjustments can make a difference.

The final and significant item affecting your retirement includes your health. At any age, health care is a priority. When you retire, however, you will probably focus more on health care than ever before. Staying healthy is your goal, and this can mean more visits to the doctor for preventive tests and routine checkups. There's also a chance that your health will decline as you grow older, increasing your need for costly prescription drugs or medical treatments. That's why having health insurance can be extremely important.

If you are 65 or older when you retire, you're most likely eligible for certain health benefits from Medicare. However, if you retire before age 65, you'll need some way to pay for your health care until Medicare kicks in. Generous employers may offer extensive health insurance coverage to their retiring employees, but this is the exception rather than the rule. If your employer doesn't extend health benefits to you, you might need to consider other options, such as buying a private health insurance policy or extending your employer-sponsored coverage through COBRA, if that's a possibility.

1) *Medicare:* Most Americans automatically become entitled to Medicare when they turn 65. In fact, if you're already receiving Social Security benefits, you won't even have to apply; you'll be automatically enrolled in Medicare. However, you will have to

decide whether you need only Part A coverage (which is premium free for most retirees) or if you also want to purchase part B coverage. Part A, commonly referred to as the hospital insurance portion of Medicare, can help pay for your home health care, hospice care, and inpatient hospital care. Part B helps cover other medical care such as physician care, laboratory tests, and physical therapy. You may also choose to enroll in a managed care plan or private fee-for-service plan under Medicare Part C (Medicare Advantage) if you want to pay fewer out-of-pocket health-care costs. If you don't already have adequate prescription drug coverage, you should also consider joining a Medicare prescription drug plan offered in your area by a private company or insurer that has been approved by Medicare.

Unfortunately, Medicare won't cover all of your health-care expenses. For some types of care, you'll have to satisfy a deductible and make co-payments. That's why many retirees purchase a Medigap policy.

2) *Medigap:* Unless you can afford to pay for the things that Medicare doesn't cover, including the annual co-payments and deductibles that apply to certain types of care, you may want to buy some type of Medigap policy when you sign up for Medicare Part B. There are 12 standard Medigap policies available. Each of these policies offers certain basic core benefits, and all but the most basic policy offer various combinations of additional benefits designed to cover what Medicare does not. Although not all Medigap plans are available in every state, you should be able to find a plan that best meets your needs and your budget.

   When you first enroll in Medicare Part B at age 65 or older, you have a six-month Medigap open enrollment period. During that time, you have a right to buy the Medigap policy of your choice from a private insurance company, regardless of any health problems you may have.

3) *Long-Term Care and Medicaid:* The possibility of a prolonged stay in a nursing home weighs heavily on the minds of many older

Americans and their families. That's hardly surprising, especially considering the high cost of long-term care. Many people look into purchasing long-term care insurance (LTCI). A good LTCI policy can cover the cost of care in a nursing home, an assisted-living facility, or even your own home. But if you're interested don't wait too long to buy it; you'll generally need to be in good health. In addition, the older you are, the higher the premium you'll pay.

Many people assume that Medicaid will pay for long-term care costs. You may be able to rely on Medicaid to pay for long-term care, but your assets and/or income must be low enough to allow you to qualify. Additionally, Medicaid eligibility rules are numerous and complicated, and varies from state to state. Talk to an attorney or financial professional who has experience with Medicaid before you make any assumptions about the role Medicaid might play in your overall plan.

Now that we have reviewed the technical aspects of retirement planning, it is critical to consider the emotional variables as well.

1) *Are you ready to retire?* The question is actually more complicated than it first appears, because it demands consideration on two levels. First, there's the emotional component . . . are you ready to enter a new phase of life? Do you have a plan for what you would like to accomplish or do in retirement? Have you thought through both the good and bad aspects of transitioning into retirement? Second, there's the financial component; can you afford to retire? Will your finances support the retirement lifestyle that you want? Do you have a retirement income plan in place? See the Retirement Checklist in Appendix H.
2) *What does retirement mean to you?* When you close your eyes and think about your retirement, what do you see? Over your career, you may have had a vague concept of retirement as a period of reward for a lifetime of hard work, full of possibility and potential. Now that retirement is approaching, though, you need to be much more specific about what it is that you want and expect in retirement.

Do you see yourself pursuing hobbies? Traveling? Have you considered volunteering your time, taking the opportunity to go back to school, or starting a new career or business? It's important that you've given it some consideration, and have a plan. If you haven't, for example, if you've thought no further than the fact that retirement simply means you won't have to go to work anymore, you're not ready to retire.

We implore you to not underestimate the emotional aspect of retirement.

Many people define themselves by their profession. Affirmation and a sense of worth may have come, in large part, from the success that you've had in your career. Giving up that career can be disconcerting on a number of levels. Consider as well the fact that your job provides a certain structure to your life. You may also have work relationships that are important to you. Without something concrete to fill the void, you may find yourself scrambling to address unmet emotional needs.

While many see retirement as a new beginning, there are some for whom retirement is seen as the transition into some "final" life stage, marking the "beginning of the end." Others, even those who have the full financial capacity to live the retirement lifestyle they desire, can't bear the thought of not receiving a regular paycheck. For these individuals, it's not necessarily the income that the paychecks represent, but the emotional reassurance of continuing to accumulate funds.

Finally, it's often not simply a question of whether you are ready to retire. If you're married, consider whether your spouse is ready for you to retire. Does he or she share your ideas of how you want to spend your retirement? Many married couples find the first few years of one or both spouse's retirement a period of rough transition. If you haven't discussed your plans with your spouse, you should do so; think through what the repercussions will be, positive and negative, on your roles and your relationship.

For a checklist on how to prepare for retirement, please see Appendix H in the back of the book.

V

Enjoy It

24

Enjoy It!

Last year, I was sitting with clients in a meeting, reviewing their accounts, catching up on their situation, etc. Towards the end of our time together I shared with them our new project: revising and adding content to our current book. After sharing the general theme of the book, including a list of the chapters, the wife of this client team rather enthusiastically said, "What about, ENJOY IT!" What a great idea! How could we have a book providing strategies of planning, growing, protecting, and distributing wealth, without mention of the reason we work so hard to achieve these goals: to enjoy life.

One of the most significant struggles doctors face is balancing the many forces grasping for their attention: work, family, finances, friends, hobbies, exercise, social events, and relaxation, among others. This being said, how does one balance all of these things and more? How does one excel at the roles of doctor, spouse, child, sibling, and friend, and still find time for the things they enjoy while also managing their finances?

Our opinion is that, with anything in life too much of any one thing is probably not healthy. Moderation and balance are the keys to holistic success. For example, if you over exercise (too hard or too often) and do not allow your body the opportunity to recover, you likely will have pain and injuries requiring medical expenditures. Too much eating or drinking alcohol can lead from good times into misery ranging from temporary discomfort like indigestion or a hangover to obesity, addiction, and the increased healthcare expenses that accompany these ailments.

Likewise, too much spending can lead to unnecessary pain in your financial life. You will face increased debt positions, additional interest costs, and the disillusioning prospect of digging yourself out of a financial hole. Alternately, too much saving/investing can also be unhealthy. For example, up until fairly recently, one of the authors of this book felt compelled to save virtually every dime. In fact, his regular "spending freezes" created a divide amongst him and his friends. Thankfully his lovely wife, business partner, and close friends, finally said, "What is the point of saving every dime if you are not going to ever enjoy your hard work?" There is much truth in their pleas: enjoying life as we live it is important too, as life offers no guarantee of longevity.

Certainly we want our clients to enjoy life too. We want our clients to have fruitful relationships doing the things they enjoy with the people they love. But, often we've found the compulsion to spend too much or not save enough stems from the desire to enjoy life now. Though we agree that enjoying life is important, without balance and moderation now, you may well be playing a stressful game of catch-up later. Clearly, the goals of retirement, education funding, etc., are important and should be planned diligently so your enjoyment of life doesn't end with a harsh wake up call.

Through the years, our observation is that many people avoid establishing a relationship with a financial advisor out of fear that the advisor's demands to save and invest all of their available money will restrict them from enjoying life. Your financial advisor, as part of your overall financial plan, should help you to identify your saving and spending objectives, and create a savings bucket for those objectives, just as you would for other goals. Plan ahead and save for your enjoyment. Ask yourself, "Can I wait to purchase this until I have the money?" OR, "Can I live without it?" If so, planning ahead for the purchase is not only financially sensible, it is emotionally comforting. A trusted financial advisor can help you identify and execute the plan that will allow you to reach your goals, while enjoying the journey as well.

VI

Conclusions

25

Should You Meet with a Financial Adviser? A Checklist

Now, after reading all of this, you may be asking one very important question . . . should I meet with a financial adviser? Below is a list of questions to consider.

- Are you without a will?
- How long has it been since you updated your will?
- Do you have family protection measures in place?
- Are you about to be married?
- Are you about to be divorced?
- Do you have a child?
- Are you planning to have a child?
- Do you have an education plan in place?
- Are you approaching the completion of training?
- Do you have an employment contract?
- Did you recently begin practicing?
- Are you about to become partner?
- Did you recently become partner?
- Did you receive 1099 income or any passive income?
- Have you sold an investment property this year (in the last 90 days)?
- Do you have non-correlating asset class investments included in your portfolio?
- Is your income protected?
- Do you have a retirement plan in place?
- Are your parents going to reduce your net worth?
- Do your parents have a retirement plan in place?
- Do your parents have Long Term Care?

- Do you have a distribution strategy for retirement?
- Is your portfolio exclusively equity-based?
- Are you concerned with litigation and its effect on achieving your goals?

26

Financial Planners—Qualities to Seek

There are a number of issues to consider and a significant of information to sort through as you move down the path towards financial independence. Do you want to spend your time researching information, developing strategies, implementing vehicles, and constantly coordinating all the efforts of investment, tax, and legal advice? A financial planner can guide you through the process, ultimately saving you valuable time and effort in coordinating these elements.

- Personality: It is critical that you feel comfortable with the planner. This will potentially be a long-term relationship, so establishing a good relationship with someone you trust is very important.
- Independent: It is essential to work with someone who can provide objective financial advice and has serving your best interests as their objective. Another way to evaluate this is to determine if there is an insurance or investment company behind or paying the planner pulling the strings or influencing advice.
- Specialist: You should be able to answer "yes" to each of the following questions. Do they understand where you've been, where you are, and where you're going? Are they intimately familiar with the issues important to doctors? Do they have a firm grasp of your desire not only to create wealth, but to protect and distribute it as well?
- Fee Planner: The planner should charge a fee for financial planning and investment advice. We have found that working with this type of planner is more likely to result in objective and unbiased advice. Types of services provided by fee planners can vary, and are specified in a financial planning agreement.

- Relationships: Most people at one point in their lives have experienced each of the following situations. First, have you ever met someone and after a period of time realized on paper they are perfect? Every item on your checklist of a prospective partner is met. However, you don't have the "it" feeling coursing through every ounce of your being. Secondly, have you ever met someone who you ONLY had the "it" feeling but on paper there was no way you would ever bring them home to your parents? In our opinion when evaluating a financial planner relationship you need both the feeling and the line item requirements for the relationship to provide maximum benefit.

27

Final Thoughts

The first step is complete. You finished reading this book.

The second step is to take action and begin taking control of your finances by following the concepts outlined. Some of you reading this book are still early in your training and perhaps feel as though you have no money. Others of you have been in practice for a number of years and maybe still feel as though you have no money, or feel that the money that you have is already allocated elsewhere. Still others of you reading this book likely feel you've addressed some of the issues mentioned but have a few holes in your financial world. No matter where you fall on the timeline, there are things you can and should do.

Start by thinking about your household budget. What could happen to your wealth by doing without or decreasing the amount of basic items: coffee, entertainment, or meals out at restaurants? Then, expand your thinking from there in terms of how simple changes to your daily lifestyle could mean more dollars in your retirement coffer!

Another step might be pursuing a second opinion about your current financial plan. If nothing else, this second opinion could help reaffirm that what you're currently doing is working toward achieving your financial goals and objectives. Make sure that your current financial team includes the right people who can assist you in developing and maintaining a comprehensive course of action.

Being Financially Healthy as far as this book is concerned isn't a random game of chance, where some people win and some people lose depending on the roll of dice or spin of a wheel. Those people who make preparations for a storm may find themselves lucky to sidestep storm damage or property loss. Those who set aside money into an emergency fund may feel lucky to have that money to pay for an unexpected car repair or medical emergency. Those who diligently save for their children's education may have lucky children who will have the opportunity to attend college and pursue more lucrative careers than their unfortunate peers. Those who care for their body with a disciplined regimen of nutrition and exercise may find themselves lucky to live long, healthy lives.

You see, though much of your future remains uncertain, there are strategies in this book that will prepare you for success no matter what the future brings. It's up to you to make a decision to create your own luck.

This is your call to action. Be proactive! Begin the process! Head towards Optimal Financial Health!

NOTES

[1] Source: 2011 IRS Tax Book

Mosaic Financial Associates

Securities and investment advisory services offered through NEXT Financial Group, Inc. Member FINRA/SIPC

Mosaic Financial Associates is not an affiliate of NEXT Financial Group, Inc.

Anthony C. Williams, ChFC, CLU, RFC
President
Investment Advisor Representative
Marc E. Ortega, ChFC, RFC
CEO
Investment Advisor Representative
VIVO Building
4650 E. Cotton Center Blvd., Suite 130
Phoenix, AZ 85040
Anthony@mosaicfa.com
Marc@mosaicfa.com

DISCLOSURES

This book has provided information on various financial topics as well as investments. Keeping in mind that everyone's financial situation is different, the strategies and concepts discussed within this book may not be appropriate for everyone. You should meet with your financial, legal and tax advisor(s) before implementing any financial, legal or tax strategy.

The tax concepts that are addressed in this book are current as of 2011. Tax laws change frequently, and any tax concept addressed in this book may not be applicable after 2011.

Legal Advice: The information, ideas, and suggestions in this book are not intended to render legal advice. Before following any suggestions contained in this book, you should consult your personal attorney. Neither the author nor the publisher shall be liable or responsible for any loss or damage allegedly arising as a consequence of your use or application of any information or suggestions in this book.

Variable Life insurance, Variable Annuities and Mutual Funds are sold only by prospectus. The prospectus contains important information about the product's charges and expenses, as well as the risks and other information associated with the product. You should carefully consider the risks, investment charges of a specific product before investing. You should always read the prospectus carefully before investing.

Anthony C. Williams and Marc E. Ortega are investment adviser representatives with NEXT Financial Group. They do not provide specific tax advice. Please consult with a tax professional before implementing any strategy.

2007 0564 MA1 DOFU 3/1/2007

APPENDIX A

	Term	Whole Life	Universal Life	Variable Life	Variable Universal Life
Premium	Premiums increase at each renewal	Level	Flexible	Level	Flexible
Coverage	Usually renewable until at least age 70; sometimes to age 95	For life	For life	For life	For life
Death benefit	Guaranteed	Guaranteed	May be guaranteed, based on policy	Guaranteed	May be guaranteed, depending on policy
		May increase with dividends*	Can be increased or decreased	Varies relative to cash value investment returns	Can be increased or decreased; varies relative to cash value investment returns
Cash value	None	Guaranteed	Guaranteed minimum interest rate	Not guaranteed	Not guaranteed
		May increase with dividends*	Varies based on interest rates	Fluctuates with subaccount performance	Fluctuates with subaccount performance
Policy loans allowed?	Not applicable	Yes	Yes	Yes	Yes
		May be able to borrow up to 100% of total cash surrender value less annual loan interest rate	Same as whole life, but usually available at lower net interest rate (i.e., pay the interest rate and get a credit back to the policy)	Same as whole life, but usually available at lower net interest rate (i.e., pay the interest rate and get a credit back to the policy)	Same as whole life, but usually available at lower net interest rate (i.e., pay the interest rate and get a credit back to the policy)
Cash withdrawals allowed?	Not applicable	No	Yes	No	Yes
Cash value account growth	No cash value account	Insurer determines guaranteed cash value and declares dividends based on performance of its general investment portfolio*	Insurer determines cash value interest crediting rates based on current interest rate returns to the company	Cash value account growth depends upon the investment performance of the subaccounts you choose	Cash value account growth depends upon the investment performance of the subaccounts you choose

*Dividends are not guaranteed.

Note: Any guarantees associated with payment of death benefits, income options, or rates of return are subject to the claims-paying ability of the insurer. Policy loans and withdrawals will reduce the policy's cash value and death benefit and may cause the policy to lapse. Withdrawals may be subject to surrender charges and income tax, and a 10% penalty may apply to withdrawals from a modified endowment contract if made under age 59 ½.

Note: Variable life and variable universal life insurance policies are offered by prospectus, which you can obtain from your financial professional or the insurance company. The prospectus contains detailed information about investment objectives, risks, charges and expenses. You should read the prospectus and consider this information carefully before purchasing a variable life or variable universal life insurance policy.

Decreasing Term

The premium remains the same while the death benefit decreases.Annual

Renewable Term

The premium will increase on an annual basis while the death benefit remains the same.

Level Term

The premium remains the same for a specified period of time: 5, 10, 15, or 20 years while the death benefit remains the same.

Cash Value—Ordinary Life or Whole Life

The premiums and death benefit remain the same while accumulating cash value on a tax-deferred basis. The uses of this type of life insurance include clearing debt, providing survivor income, and paying estate taxes.

Universal Life

The premiums and death benefit are flexible while accumulating cash value on a tax-deferred basis. The benefits and uses are very similar to Whole Life while providing an opportunity for enhanced cash value accumulation.

Indexed Life

The premiums and death benefit are flexible while accumulating cash value on a tax-advantaged basis. You are not invested in the market; rather your accumulation occurs via crediting according to various indexes. There is a cap on the down and upside.

Variable Life

The premiums and death benefit may be adjusted, while accumulating cash value on a tax-deferred basis. The accumulation is directly impacted by market performance, specifically the type of investment option chosen, such as stock funds, bond funds, money market funds, etc.

Single Premium Life

One premium is paid at issue of contract with a level minimum death benefit while accumulating cash value.

First to Die

The premium may adjust while maintaining a minimum level death benefit on two or more parties. The death benefit is received at the first death.

Survivorship Life/Second-to-die

The premium may adjust while maintaining a minimum level death benefit on two people. The death benefit is paid at the second death.

APPENDIX B

Wrap Accounts

What is a wrap account?

The term "wrap account" typically refers to an account that offers unlimited transactions within the account and charges a quarterly or annual fee (usually a percentage of the assets in the account) that covers all investing costs, including any trading costs. A wrap account typically offers suggestions about how to invest those assets based on your investment objectives and risk tolerance.

How does it generally work?

When you decide to establish a wrap account, you (the client) will typically sit down with a financial professional and map out an investment plan based on your risk tolerance and financial objectives. The broker then selects a professional money manager (or managers) who select an appropriate mix of mutual funds that match your needs. The money manager may work independently or in-house for your brokerage firm, but either way, he or she works through your broker.

How does a wrap account generally work?

There are generally two types of wrap accounts. A mutual fund wrap account is made up of only mutual funds, usually more than one. The selection of those funds typically is based on a computerized asset allocation mode that takes into account your financial objectives, age, risk tolerance, and investing time horizon. The portfolio is typically rebalanced periodically to maintain the agreed-on asset allocation. (Similar types of wrap accounts that focus on using exchange-traded funds (ETFs) also exist.)

A nondiscretionary advisory account is a type of wrap account offered by brokerage houses which can hold a broader range of investments—for example, individual stocks and bonds, mutual funds, exchange-traded funds, and cash alternatives. An individual advisor can make asset allocation and investment recommendations as well as monitor your portfolio, but is not allowed to make final decisions without your authorization.

> **Technical Note:** Because of a 2007 U.S. Court of Appeals decision, fee-based brokerage accounts that include investment recommendations may be offered only if they are managed by a registered investment advisor (who may be part of the same firm as the broker).

A nondiscretionary advisory account is different from a separately managed account, in which an investment advisor selects one or more money managers to handle individual investments held in the account but which is typically focused on one asset class.

What are the costs of a wrap account?

Most mutual fund companies offer wrap programs with a minimum investment of between $10,000 and $15,000. But that minimum investment standard is changing. Because of the popularity of wrap accounts, "mini" wraps are appearing among financial houses to attract investors who have smaller portfolios. The wrap fees usually range between 2.5 percent and 3.5 percent of assets annually. Mutual fund wrap accounts tend to offer lower fees; however, if a fund wrap account charges a sales commission, you may have to pay a front-end load when you buy or be liable for a redemption fee when you sell. There may also be underlying mutual fund feeds in addition to the wrap fee itself.

Strengths

Investment Recommendations

A wrap account gives you access to professional investment expertise. This is a distinct advantage for mutual fund investors who may have substantial assets but little time, inclination, or desire to develop and monitor their asset allocation strategy themselves.

Eliminates Incentive to Churn Account

Because commissions are not paid each time securities are bought and sold, the financial professional you work with has no reason to make trades simply to increase commissions. The more actively the account is managed, the greater the advantage of eliminating commissions in favor of a flat fee.

Tradeoffs

May Provide Unnecessary Services

If you anticipate that your account will not involve frequent trading, it may be more cost-effective to pay per-trade commissions or sales charges in a regular mutual fund or traditional brokerage account. Also, if you are comfortable with your own understanding of and experience with investments and investing strategy, investment recommendations may not be useful enough to justify a wrap account's fee.

Lack of Flexibility

Your choice of funds in a mutual fund wrap account may be limited to proprietary in-house funds, or just a handful of funds.

APPENDIX C

Legal Documents to Consider

PROBATE
Probate is the process of transferring your assets to your heirs through the court system.

WILLS
A Will provides a simple means to pass your estate to your heirs. It serves as instructions to the Probate Court to appoint and supervise your selected Executor in the location, collection and inventorying of assets, paying creditors, and distributing the estate to your heirs.

POWER OF ATTORNEY (General Durable, Medical or Limited)
A Power of Attorney grants legal authority to manage your financial affairs, and to make medical decisions during a disability. It can also be restricted to specific events. These documents avoid the expense of guardianship and conservatorship proceedings in the event that you become disabled.

LIVING WILL (Physician's Directive)
When coupled with a Medical Power of Attorney, a Living Will advises your physician and family of your decision, if you become terminally ill, that your death or suffering not be prolonged by medical technology.

TRUST (Revocable, Irrevocable, or Testamentary)
A trust is a contract for the management of assets. It instructs a Trustee(s) to manage property for the benefit of your beneficiaries. The plan may survive death or disability of one or both spouses. Additionally, it may help avoid estate taxes.

LIVING TRUST

A Living Trust avoids probate on assets owned in trust at the death of each spouse. It is managed by a person(s) you choose if you are disabled. It is not a matter of public record, and avoids the expense of a probate proceeding.

ADVANCED ESTATE PLANNING

There are many techniques to reduce or eliminate estate taxes. A good plan will be a combination of planning theories and strategies that specifically meet your financial and non-financial objectives and goals.

Each individual need is different. To avoid pitfalls that improper planning and documentation can inadvertently produce, you should investigate the legal tools that best fit your estate management needs. The choices you make, however, should be based on a thorough understanding of your legal options.

APPENDIX D

Mutual Fund Basics

What is it?

A mutual fund is an investment company that pools money from many people and invests it in stocks, bonds, or other securities. Each investor owns shares, which represents a part of these holdings. Investors can buy shares (or portions) directly from the fund of through brokers, banks, financial planning professionals, or insurance agents. All mutual funds will redeem (buy back) your shares on any business day and must send you the payment within seven days.

When you buy shares, you pay the current net asset value (NAV), the value of one share in a fund per share, plus any sales charge (known as a sales load). When you sell your shares, the fund will pay you NAV less any other contingent deferred sales charge (CDSC). As with individual stocks, the share price of mutual funds fluctuates daily and the value of an investment may be more or less than its original cost.

Mutual funds can be a great way to invest because . . .

- They are a collection of many stocks, and/or bonds, so your investment risk is spread out (keep in mind that, as with all investments, mutual funds carry risks)
- They are managed by professional fund managers who invest the pooled money into individual securities
- Costs associated with the underlying security are often lower than what you would pay on your own because the fund buys and sells large amounts of securities at one time.

Caution: Mutual funds are not guaranteed or insured by any bank or government agency—even mutual funds sold by banks.

How do investors make money with mutual funds?

Money is made from a mutual fund when the stocks, bonds, or other securities increase in value or issue dividends.

- The net asset value (NAV) of the securities a fund owns may increase. When a fund sells a security that has increased in NAV, the fund has a capital gain. At the end of the year, most funds distribute these capital gains (minus any capital losses) to investors.
- If a fund does not sell but holds on to securities that have increased in value, the fund's NAV increases. If you sell your shares, you make a profit (capital gain).
- A fund may receive income in the form of dividends and interest on the securities it owns and pass it along to the fund's shareholders.

Usually, you can accept payment for distributions and dividends, or you can reinvest them in the fund, often without paying an additional sales charge.

How can taxes affect mutual funds?

Taxes can significantly reduce the net returns on your mutual fund investment, so you should pay close attention to them.

Tax-Exempt Bond Funds

Some bond funds invest in municipal bonds that pay interest which is exempt from federal income taxes. In addition, interest on the bonds of some states is exempt from taxation by that state. Not all of the income you receive from a municipal bond fund, however, will necessarily be exempt from federal or state income tax. The fund's prospectus will describe any of its tax-exempt features. Source http://www.sec.gov/answers/bondfunds.htm

Tax-Efficient Funds

One of the objectives of tax-efficient mutual funds is to keep shareholder tax liability to a minimum. For example, a fund may attempt to minimize trading that generates capital gains, which would require shareholders to pay taxes if the fund is held in a taxable account.

Nontaxable Return of Capital

It's possible for a mutual fund to make a distribution to you without your having to pay tax on it. This generally occurs when a distribution involves recovery of all or a portion of your cost basis (i.e. the amount of your investment) in the fund. Such a distribution is not subject to taxation because it does not represent investment earnings. It still must be reported on your tax return, however.

Income from Dividends

Many funds pay dividends on a monthly, quarterly, or annual basis. Dividends are distributed to shareholders on a pro rata basis. They must be reported on your return (whether reinvested or paid in cash) in the year of distribution.

For tax years beginning on or after January 1, 2003 and before January 1, 2011, qualifying dividends paid to individual shareholders from domestic corporations (and qualified foreign corporations) are taxed at long-term capital gains tax rates. (In tax years prior to January 1, 2003, stock dividends were taxed at ordinary income tax rates, generally resulting in significantly higher tax liability.)

> **Caution:** Absent further legislative action, stock dividends will again be taxed as ordinary income beginning in 2011.

However, dividends from mutual funds to individual shareholders may or may not quality for taxation at capital gains rates. In general, qualifying corporate stock dividends that a mutual fund receives and passes through to its own shareholders qualify for taxation at capital gains rates. To the extent those mutual fund dividends are attributable to other types of earnings (e.g., interest), however, the dividends will be taxed as ordinary income.

Caution: When it comes to dividends qualifying for long-term capital gain tax treatment, special holding period requirements apply to mutual fund shareholders. For stock dividends to qualify for taxation at the long-term capital gain tax rates, the stock must generally be held for at least 61 days during the 121-day period beginning 60 days before the ex-dividend date. Mutual funds that hold dividend-paying stock and meet this requirement may pass through qualifying dividends to mutual fund shareholders. However, mutual fund shareholders must themselves hold their mutual fund shares for at least 61 days during the 121 day period beginning 60 days before the mutual fund shares' ex-dividend rate to be able to take advantage of the lower capital gain rates on the dividends that are passed through.

Example(s): (From IRS Publication 550) You bought 10,000 shares of ABC Mutual Fund common stock on July 1. ABC Mutual Fund paid a cash dividend of 10 cents per share. The ex-dividend date was July 9. The ABC Mutual Fund advises you that the portion of the dividend eligible to be treated as qualified dividends equals 2 cents per share. Your Form 1099-DIV from ABC Mutual Fund shows total ordinary dividends of $1,000 and qualified dividends of $200. However, you sold the 10,000 shares on August 4. You have no qualified dividends from ABC Mutual Fund, because you did not hold the ABC Mutual Fund stock for more than 60 days.

Short-Term Capital Gains

Short-term capital gain distributions (representing the fund's net gains from the sale of securities held in its portfolio for one year or less) made by a fund are generally treated the same as dividends for tax purposes.

Long-Term Capital Gains

Long-term capital gain distributions (representing the fund's net gains from the sale of securities held in its portfolio for more than one year) are made to the fund's shareholders on a pro rata basis. Shareholders must report the amount distributed in their tax returns as long as a long-term capital gain (regardless of how long the shares have been held) is subject to capital gains tax rates.

Sales of Shares

When you redeem shares of a fund, you generally must pay tax on any capital gain realized. The taxable amount of the gain, if any, will generally be equal to the difference between the sale price and the price for which you originally purchased the shares. The amount of tax to be paid on a gain depends on the rate at which the gain is taxed, which in turn depends on how long you owned the fund shares prior to selling them. Generally speaking, when you sell shares after holding them for more than a year, any gain from the sale will be a long-term capital gain. In contrast, if you sell shares that you owned for a year or less, any resulting gain will be a short-term capital gain, taxed at ordinary income tax rates. Since long-term capital gains rates are generally more favorable than ordinary income tax rates, the same gain can produce different tax liabilities depending on the holding period.

> **Tip:** Keep in mind that capital losses from other investments can be used to offset capital gains. These losses can even be carried forward and used to offset gains in future years.

Exchange of Shares

An exchange of shares from one fund to another is generally treated the same as a sale of shares for tax purposes.

What are the costs associated with mutual funds?

Like taxes, mutual fund fees and expenses are important because they have an impact on your net returns. Here are some of the common costs associated with mutual funds:

- Sales loads and transaction feeds (paid when you buy, sell, or exchange your shares)

- Ongoing expenses, such as 12b-1 fees and management fees (paid while you remain invested in the fund)

Caution: High expenses do not ensure superior performance.

Tip: A fund's costs are laid out in the fee table near the front of the fund's prospectus. You can use the fee tables to compare the costs of different funds.

What types of mutual funds are there?

There are several major types of mutual funds. Most mutual funds invest in one of the three major asset classes: equities (stocks), fixed income (bonds), and cash equivalents (money market instruments). There are many variations within these three main categories. There are also funds that combine multiple types of investments. For example, asset allocation funds combine all three major asset classes. Some funds invest in other mutual funds rather than individual securities (a so-called fund of funds, for example).

In addition to these securities in which they invest, mutual funds may be categorized by their investing strategy. For example, tax-efficient funds strive to minimize investors' tax liability. Some funds are actively managed; others simply attempt to replicate an index.

Index Disclosure: An index is a composite of securities that provides a performance benchmark. Returns are presented for illustrative purposes only and are not intended to project the performance of any specific investment. Indexes are unmanaged, do not incur management fees, costs and expenses and cannot be invested in directly.

How do you choose a mutual fund?

Each type of mutual fund has different risks and rewards. Generally, the higher the potential return, the higher the risk of loss. Shop around. Compare a mutual fund with others of the same type. Decide whether the goals and risks of any fund you are considering are a good fit for you. Before investing in a mutual fund, carefully consider its investment objectives, risks, fees, and expenses, which can be found in the prospectus available from the fund. Read it carefully before investing. Don't hesitate to get expert help if all the information leaves you overwhelmed, or if you'd prefer to have someone else do the detailed research for you.

APPENDIX E

Alternative Asset Classes

What are alternative asset classes?

Beyond the three primary asset classes: stocks, bonds, and cash, many other types of investments can be used to diversify investment portfolios. The term "alternative assets" is highly flexible. It may include specific physical assets, such as natural resources or real estate, or methods of investing, such as hedge funds or private equity. In some cases, even geographic regions, such as emerging global markets, are considered alternative assets.

Alternative assets often are highly dependent on novel investing strategies or individual skill in selecting specific investments. For example, hedge funds (see below) exist to pursue investing strategies that often rely on the manager's judgment and that may be difficult or impossible for a mutual fund; with collectibles such as art or antiques, the value of your investment depends on the properties of a specific work. As a result, even if you are very knowledgeable about a specific asset class, you might do well to seek out expert advice and guidance when selecting alternative assets for inclusion in your portfolio.

Why invest in alternative asset classes?

Their lack of correlation with other types of investments may help increase or stabilize portfolio return.

Part of sound portfolio management is diversifying investments (* **DIVERSIFICATION** does not guarantee against market losses. It is a method used to help manage investment risk.) so that if one type of investment is performing poorly, another may be doing well.

Both institutional and individual investors have increasingly begun to explore alternative assets in recent years as a way of trying to increase returns and/or diversify risk. In a global economy, traditional asset classes such as stocks and bonds are increasingly linked. However, in many cases, an alternative asset's performance is often highly dependent on the qualities of the individual investment, as opposed to being highly correlated to an overall market. In other cases, such as precious metals, the asset class as a whole may behave differently from stocks and bonds.

Many alternative investments attempt to achieve their returns not from the activity of the market but by using unique investing strategies to exploit market inefficiencies that the markets haven't perceived. As a result, alternative assets can provide an additional layer of diversification and complement more traditional asset classes. However, diversification alone cannot guarantee a profit or ensure against a loss. While alternative assets offer potential for returns that aren't highly correlated with other markets, their unique properties also mean that they can involve a high degree of risk.

They can take advantage of different or relaxed regulatory provisions.

Hedge funds have greater latitude than mutual funds in pursuing investing strategies, and have had to provide less disclosure to investors. This greater freedom gives them capabilities that may be off-limits to other investment companies, such as selling securities short. It also reduces the chance that a proprietary strategy may be adopted by competitors or become so widely known that it loses any market advantage.

They may provide pride of ownership.

In addition to their investment value, some alternative investments, such as art, antiques or gems, may simply be a pleasure to own. Also, certain types of alternative assets, such as revenue from timber harvests may receive favorable tax treatment.

Tradeoffs

Alternative assets often are less liquid than stocks or bonds.

Depending on the alternative asset, you may or may not be able to find a willing buyer when you're ready to sell. Also, some hedge funds may require investors to stay invested for a certain period of time.

Accurately assessing values and risks may be difficult.

The performance of an alternative asset can be challenging to research, price, and understand.

You may not have access to a given investment.

Unless you meet suitability requirements for investing, including income level and minimum investment, you may not be permitted to invest in a hedge fund.

Greater investing freedom can increase potential for mismanagement or loss from sector exposure.

Because they are subject to less regulation than many other investments, there are fewer constraints to prevent potential manipulation or to limit risk from highly concentrated positions in a single investment. Also, hard assets such as bullion, antiques, art or gems are subject to physical risk and may involve special considerations such as storage and insurance, while timberland may be subject to natural disasters.

Hedge funds

Hedge funds are private investment vehicles that manage money for institutions and wealthy individuals. They generally are organized as limited partnerships, with the fund managers as general partners and the investors as limited partners. The general partner may receive a percentage of the assets, additional fees based on performance, or both. Hedge funds originally derived their name from their ability to hedge against a market downturn by selling short. Though they may invest in stocks and bonds, hedge funds are typically considered an alternative asset class because of their ability to implement complex investing strategies that involve many other asset classes and investments.

Private Equity

Like stock shares, private equity represents an ownership interest in a company. However, unlike stocks, private equity investments are not listed or traded on a public market or exchange, and private equity firms often are more directly involved with management of the business than the average shareholder. Private equity often requires a long-term focus before investments begin to produce any meaningful cash flow, if indeed they ever do. Private equity also typically requires a relatively large investment and is available only to qualified investors such as pension funds, institutional investors and wealthy individuals. Private equity can take many forms. The following are some examples.

- Angel investors are individual investors who provide capital to startup companies and may have a personal stake in the venture, providing business expertise, industry experience and contacts as well as capital.
- Venture capital funds invest in companies that are in the early to mid-growth stages of their development and may not yet have a meaningful cash flow. In exchange, the venture capital fund receives a stake in the company.
- Mezzanine financing occurs when private investors agree to lend money to an established company in exchange for a stake in the company if the debt is not completely repaid on time. It is often used to finance expansion or acquisitions and is typically subordinated to other debt. As a result, from an investor's standpoint, mezzanine financing can be rewarding because the interest paid to the investor on the loan is often high.
- Buyouts occur when private investors, often part of a private equity fund, purchase all or part of a public company and take it private, believing that either the company is undervalued or that they can improve the company's profitability and sell it later at a higher price. In some cases, the private investors are the company's executives, and the buyout is known as a "management buyout (MBO)." A "leveraged buyout (LBO)" is financed not only with investor capital but with bonds issued by the private equity group to pay for purchase of the outstanding stock.

Real Estate

You may make either direct or indirect investments in buildings either commercial or residential and/or land. Direct investment involves the purchase, improvement, and/or rental of property; indirect investments are made through an entity that invests in property, such as a real estate investment trust (REIT). Real estate has a relatively low correlation with the behavior of the stock market and is often viewed as a hedge against inflation.

Natural Resources

Most investments in natural resources such as timber, oil or natural gas are done through limited partnerships. In some cases, such as timber, the resource replenishes itself; in other cases, such as oil or natural gas, the resource may be depleted over time. Timberland produces income from the trees harvested, but may also grow in value and be converted for use as a real estate development.

Art, Antiques, Gems and Collectibles

Some investors are drawn to investment-grade collectibles because they may retain their value or even appreciate as inflation rises. If you are a knowledgeable collector or have expert advice, they may generate high returns. However, their value can be unpredictable and can be affected by supply and demand, economic conditions, and the condition of an individual piece or collection.

Gold and Precious Metals

Investors have traditionally purchased precious metals such as gold, silver, platinum, and palladium because they believe that precious metals provide security in times of economic and social upheaval. Gold, for instance, has historically been seen as an alternative to paper currency and therefore a hedge against inflation and currency fluctuations. If paper currency becomes worth less and less because of inflation, investors perceive that gold will retain its value. As a result, gold prices often rise when investors are worried that the dollar is losing value. However, the price of gold is volatile; its value may rise and then fall quickly. In recent years, the price of gold has been particularly difficult to predict and has shown little correlation with inflation. There are many ways to invest in precious metals. In addition to buying bullion or coins, you can also invest in futures, shares in mining companies, sector funds, and exchange-traded funds.

Commodities and Financial Futures

Commodities are physical substances that are fundamental to the creation of other products or to commerce generally. Unlike most other products that are bought and sold, a commodity is basically indistinguishable from any other commodity of the same type. Examples of commodities include oil and natural gas, agricultural products (such as corn, wheat, and soybeans), livestock (such as cattle and hogs), and metals (such as copper, nickel and zinc).

Commodities are typically traded through futures contracts. Futures are contractual agreements that promise future delivery of something upon a certain date, at a specified price. For example, a commodities futures contract might involve wheat, corn, oil or natural gas, among others. Futures contracts also are available for financial instruments, such as a stock index or a currency. Futures contracts are standardized and are traded on organized exchanges. Although the futures market was originally created to facilitate trading among individuals and companies who produce, own, or use commodities in their businesses, the market has expanded to include individuals and companies that buy and sell futures contracts as a way of investing.

Like options, futures are considered derivatives because their value is based on some other security. Futures allow an investor to leverage a relatively small amount of capital. However, they can be highly speculative and are not suitable for all investors.

APPENDIX F

Traditional Investments

- Stocks
  When you buy a company's stock, you're purchasing a share of ownership in that business. You become one of the company's stockholders or shareholders. Your percentage of ownership in a company also represents your share of the risks taken and profits generated by the company. If the company does well, your share of its earnings will be proportionate to how much of the company's stock you own. The flip side, of course, is that your share of any loss will be similarly proportionate to your percentage of ownership.

- Bonds
  When you buy a bond, you're basically buying an IOU. Bonds, sometimes called fixed-income securities, are essentially loans to a corporation or governmental body. The borrower (the bond issuer) typically promises to pay the lender, or bondholder, regular interest payments until a certain date. At that point, the bond is said to have matured. When it reaches that maturity date, the full amount of the loan (the principal or face value) must be repaid.

- Cash
  In daily life, cash is all around you as currency, bank balances, negotiable money orders, and checks. However, in investing, "cash" is also used to refer to so-called cash alternatives: investments that are considered safe and can be converted to cash quickly. Common cash alternatives include savings accounts, money market deposit accounts, money market funds, certificates of deposit, guaranteed investment contracts (GICs), government savings bonds, U.S.

Treasury bills, Eurodollar certificates of deposit, commercial paper, and face amount certificates.

- Mutual Funds and ETFs
  You can invest in all three major asset classes through mutual funds, which pool your money with that of other investors. Each fund's manager selects specific securities to buy based on a stated investment strategy.

APPENDIX G

Separately Managed And Unified Managed Accounts

Tailored to Suit You

For investors who want or need a relatively customized and tax-efficient approach to creating a diversified investment portfolio, separately managed and unified managed accounts may help them achieve that goal.

What is a separately managed account?

A separately managed account (SMA) is a portfolio of assets that are managed by one or more professional money managers. (SMAs can also be known as individually managed accounts, separate accounts, or privately managed accounts). In an SMA, your assets are not commingled with those of other investors, as they are with a mutual fund. When you buy shares of a mutual fund, each fund share represents a proportionate ownership of each individual security within the fund, even though your ownership stake in each security is tiny. With a separately managed account, you are the sole owner of each security held within your separately managed account. You also can place securities you already own in your SMA; with mutual funds, you can't.

As a result, you and your financial professional have more control over management of specific investments in an SMA. Why is that important; because it increases your ability to coordinate the sale of specific securities with the rest of your overall financial plan. However, don't expect to micromanage every single trade, as you might with a traditional brokerage account. An SMA's overall investing strategy and securities selection often is based on a proprietary model developed by the investment management firm that operates it. Within that model and the guidelines you set, the money manager for your SMA typically will have discretion to implement strategies that the manager feels will provide the best returns for you. (After all, if you want to make all the decisions yourself, it probably doesn't make sense to hire a professional money manager).

Advantages

- You can exclude specific securities or sectors. For example, if you work for a large company that is a mainstay of most large-cap stock indexes, and you also hold shares in the company as a result of having exercised stock options, you might instruct your SMA's manager not to buy your company's stock to prevent your net worth from being too dependent on one company. Also, if you prefer not to invest in a specific industry, for example, tobacco or casino stocks, you can have them excluded from your SMA.
- You have the flexibility to integrate decisions made within an SMA with the rest of your financial concerns. For example, if you will owe capital gains on another account, you might decide to sell a security within your SMA to recognize a capital loss that can offset those capital gains.
- You can track the purchase, sale and cost basis of individual securities. Your statement will reflect each and every security your SMA holds.
- SMAs offer greater potential for tax efficiency. Each security held in an SMA has an individual cost basis. That allows you to make specific tax-motivated moves. As noted previously, you can generally request that your SMA's manager harvest tax losses in specific securities in order to offset capital gains, thus reducing your income tax liability.

Tradeoffs

- Because of their customization and the fact that they are of most benefit to relatively affluent investors, SMAs often have high minimum balances. Depending on the minimum balance required for a given SMA, the amount needed to invest in multiple asset classes could be substantial.
- An SMA can be challenging to research. Unlike a mutual fund, an SMA is not required to supply potential investors

with a prospectus that supplies standardized information about investment objectives, risks, fees, and expenses, which you should consider prior to investing in a mutual fund. As a result, due diligence must be performed to learn about an SMA's performance, investing approach and process, expenses (including the manager's compensation), and transaction costs. Much of this information is available from the Form ADV that SMA managers are required to file with the SEC (Securities and Exchange Commission) and the manager's disclosure documents. A financial professional can be extremely useful in doing this level of detailed research.

- Because of the relatively customized management of an SMA, fees may be higher than they would be for a similar mutual fund. It's important to weigh those fees against the tax benefits you expect to derive from an SMA.

Comparing trading costs, fees, and performance of SMAs and mutual funds.

Unlike traditional brokerage accounts, which are commission-based, SMA fee structures are asset-based. They typically cover the investment management fee, trading costs, custody, reporting, and financial planning services. Generally speaking, the larger your account, the more likely you are to benefit from an SMA.

One thing to consider when comparing mutual fund expenses against SMA fees is the "invisible" trading costs incurred by mutual funds. Mutual fund expense ratios cover fund management fees, administrative costs, and other operating expenses. However, they don't cover trading costs, which include brokerage commissions whenever the fund buys or sells securities. Although these trading costs can vary significantly by mutual fund (depending in large part on a fund's annual turnover rate), estimates of these costs often range anywhere from 0.5 percent to 1 percent.

What is a Unified Managed Account?

Unified Managed Accounts (UMAs) are an outgrowth of the separately managed account concept. They offer a more efficient way to manage the asset allocation process and integrate a variety of investment vehicles. A separately managed account typically has a single investment manager (or management firm), and often invests in only one type of asset, equities, for example. A unified managed account allows you (or your financial professional) to aggregate multiple asset managers and investment vehicles within one account, and make investment decisions in the context of a much broader view of your overall finances.

For example, a unified managed account might include a separately managed account, individual securities (including restricted securities), one or more mutual funds or exchange-traded funds, a portfolio managed by an individual advisor, and other registered investment products. (Individual firms may set their own limits on the types of holdings a UMA may include.) This allows the investor to determine an appropriate asset allocation, address tax issues, rebalance a portfolio across all those various holdings, and manage cash flow more strategically across investment products.

The more complex your financial life and the greater your assets, the more benefit you may get from a UMA.

How Unified Managed Accounts Work

A UMA may allow investors to select a predetermined asset allocation; the UMA is then managed on an individual basis to maintain that asset allocation. Or, it may offer customized modeling of a portfolio and asset allocation that is tailored to a specific individual.

A UMA has several components. The most fundamental level is the investment management of individual components of the account (sometimes referred to as individual "sleeves"). Those individual components may be combined and transactions executed by another firm (this is sometimes referred to as the "overlay" function). In most cases, the overlay portfolio manager manages the overall strategy and actual execution of cross-investment transactions (for example, tax-loss harvesting) based on models developed by the individual investment managers; in some cases, the portfolio-level investment management decisions are made jointly by the overlay portfolio manager and the sponsoring firm that deals directly with the individual investor.

Technical Note: In some cases, the individual investment manager retains discretion over both the investment model and client accounts.

This is the most similar to a separately managed account. However, most UMAs today follow one of the two procedures outlined above.

Advantages

- Enhanced ability to manage taxes. Because a UMA provides a more holistic understanding of your financial assets, it can simplify the process of a managing tax loss harvesting across multiple assets.
- Enhanced ability to manage an overall asset allocation across multiple managers and asset classes. Because a variety of different assets can be viewed and considered simultaneously, a UMA produces a more unified view of your finances, and facilitates a more accurate asset allocation strategy. Also, it streamlines the process of rebalancing a portfolio to achieve a given asset allocation. Your financial professional has a greater ability to determine exactly which securities would be most beneficial to adjust, because a UMA gives a broader perspective on your overall assets.
- Greater ability to monitor performance at the portfolio level rather than at the individual investment level.
- Enhanced ability to manage cash balances across multiple "sleeves". For example, a UMA could have a sleeve specifically set up to handle regular cash disbursements, which is replenished automatically by dividends or income from another sleeve.
- Convenience. Because multiple investment vehicles and accounts can be included within a single account, a UMA eliminates the need for multiple statements. Instead of receiving separate statements from a separately managed account, a brokerage account, and two or three various fund companies, you can view all of them in a single document.
- Enhanced ability to monitor tax concerns. A UMA can coordinate transactions in various sleeves so that you don't inadvertently violate tax regulations, such as those governing wash sales.

Tradeoffs

- Unified managed accounts typically are most beneficial for individuals with a relatively high net worth, for whom sophisticated tax management strategies are a key concern.
- The greater the degree of customization, the higher a UMA's fee is likely to be, because the complexity of making investment decisions and trades that involve multiple managers is likely to be greater.

APPENDIX H

Are you ready to retire? (Checklist)

General information	**Yes**	**No**	**N/A**
1. Has relevant personal information been gathered? • Age • Age of spouse or partner • Number of minor children and their ages	❑	❑	❑
2. Has financial situation been assessed? • Estimated annual expenses during retirement • Estimated annual income during retirement (pretax and after-tax) • Total assets and savings to date • Total retirement savings to date • Estimated yearly contribution to retirement savings • Total liabilities to date • Income tax bracket and filing status • Health insurance coverage for each spouse • Long-term care insurance coverage for each spouse • Life insurance coverage for each spouse • Wills, durable power of attorney, health-care proxy, and other estate planning information • Beneficiary designations	❑	❑	❑
Notes:			
Determining retirement income needs	**Yes**	**No**	**N/A**

1. Has life expectancy been estimated to project how long retirement will last?	❑	❑	❑
2. Have clear goals and objectives been established for retirement?	❑	❑	❑
3. Have other major financial goals been funded or achieved? • Pay off home mortgage • Fund children's education • Buy retirement home • Other	❑	❑	❑
4. If not, have those other goals been prioritized with retirement goals?	❑	❑	❑
5. Have annual retirement expenses been estimated, keeping in mind that those expenses may change from year to year? • Food, clothing, housing • Insurance • Health care • Travel and recreation • Other	❑	❑	❑
6. Have annual retirement income needs been estimated, based on the preceding goals and expenses?	❑	❑	❑
7. Has expected annual income been estimated, and will that income be sufficient to meet retirement needs? • Social Security • Pensions • Savings and investments (including IRAs and retirement plans) • Job earnings • Other	❑	❑	❑
8. If not, are there steps that can be taken to bridge the gap? • Work part-time • Cut expenses • Set more modest goals • Delay retirement • Other	❑	❑	❑

9. Have inflation, taxes, and conservative rates of return been factored into these estimates?	❑	❑	❑
Notes:			
Employer-sponsored retirement plans and IRAs	**Yes**	**No**	**N/A**
1. Is a 401(k) or other employer-sponsored retirement plan funded?	❑	❑	❑
2. Is an IRA in place? • Roth IRAs • Traditional IRAs	❑	❑	❑
3. Are the tax issues associated with taking distributions from IRAs and employer-sponsored plans understood?	❑	❑	❑
4. Has leaving money in these retirement accounts as long as possible to defer taxes and prolong tax-deferred growth been considered?	❑	❑	❑
Notes:			
Annuities and other savings tools	**Yes**	**No**	**N/A**
1. Are there annuities, or has thought been given to purchasing annuities?	❑	❑	❑
2. If so, is the taxation of annuities and the payout options available understood?	❑	❑	❑
3. Have a payout option and payment beginning date been chosen?	❑	❑	❑
4. Are there other savings tools owned, whether part of the retirement portfolio or not? • Cash value life insurance • Mutual funds • Stocks and bonds • CDs • Other	❑	❑	❑

5. If so, are the tax issues surrounding these tools understood?	❑	❑	❑
Notes:			

Investment planning	**Yes**	**No**	**N/A**
1. Now that retirement is here (or near), have plans been made to change how the retirement portfolio and other assets are invested?	❑	❑	❑
2. Will the client/advisor monitor the retirement portfolio and other investments throughout retirement and make changes when appropriate?	❑	❑	❑
3. Have expectations been established for how the retirement portfolio and other investments will perform in the coming years?	❑	❑	❑
4. Is some degree of investment risk acceptable to the client?	❑	❑	❑
5. Has a distribution strategy been discussed/developed?	❑	❑	❑
Notes:			

Insurance planning	**Yes**	**No**	**N/A**
1. If under age 65, will adequate health insurance be available until Medicare eligibility is established?	❑	❑	❑
2. If 65 or older, has a Medigap or other health policy been purchased to supplement Medicare, or is employer-sponsored coverage available?	❑	❑	❑
3. Is there long-term care insurance, or have this and other strategies been considered to protect against the cost of nursing home care?	❑	❑	❑
4. Have life insurance needs been revisited?	❑	❑	❑

<table>
<tr><td>5. Have other types of insurance coverage been reviewed?
• Auto and homeowners
• Disability (will end at retirement)
• Liability
• Other</td><td>❑</td><td>❑</td><td>❑</td></tr>
<tr><td colspan="4">Notes:</td></tr>
<tr><th>Estate planning</th><th>Yes</th><th>No</th><th>N/A</th></tr>
<tr><td>1. Will beneficiary designations be reviewed periodically?
• Employer-sponsored plans
• IRAs
• Annuities
• Life insurance
• Other</td><td>❑</td><td>❑</td><td>❑</td></tr>
<tr><td>2. Has will been reviewed/updated?</td><td>❑</td><td>❑</td><td>❑</td></tr>
<tr><td>3. Is there a durable power of attorney or health-care proxy?</td><td>❑</td><td>❑</td><td>❑</td></tr>
<tr><td>4. Have other estate planning tools and strategies been considered?
• Trusts
• Gifting assets
• Durable power of attorneys
• Advanced medical directives
• Other</td><td>❑</td><td>❑</td><td>❑</td></tr>
<tr><td colspan="4">Notes:</td></tr>
</table>

APPENDIX I

Understanding Tax Brackets
Referenced on page 50

What is ordinary income?

Ordinary income is income that is taxed at ordinary income tax rates and does not qualify for capital gains tax treatment. It's important to understand the difference between ordinary income and capital gain income because, generally, ordinary income tax rates are higher than capital gains tax rates.

It may be easier to understand what ordinary income is by understanding what it is not; it is not capital gain income from the sale or exchange of assets, or income from the sale of certain property used in a trade or business (Section 1231 property).

Ordinary income can be derived from:

- Wages, salaries, tips, and other employment compensation
- Interest earned on savings and investments
- Alimony
- Business and farm income
- Taxable portions of distributions from IRAs, retirement plans, and annuities
- Rents and royalties
- Unemployment compensation
- Taxable portions of Social Security payments
- Gambling winnings

In order to understand how ordinary income affects your tax liability, you should know what ordinary income is, how it is taxed, when it is preferable to capital gain income, and how to accelerate or defer the recognition of ordinary income.

Caution: Prior to 2003, dividends from corporate stock were classified as ordinary income. Under the Jobs and Growth Tax Relief Reconciliation Act of 2003 and the Tax Increase Prevention and Reconciliation Act of 2005, qualifying dividends paid to individual shareholders are taxed at long-term capital gains tax rates. This change in the law is effective for tax years 2003 through 2010. In 2011, absent further legislative action, the law reverts to pre-2003 Tax Act status (i.e., corporate dividends will be classified as ordinary income).

Taxation of Ordinary Income

Generally speaking and with limitations, ordinary income is reduced by ordinary losses and deductions. The balance is taxed at ordinary income tax rates. Ordinary income rates tend to be less favorable than long-term capital gains tax rates. As a result, investors generally prefer long-term capital gains to ordinary income. However, there are times when ordinary income may produce a more favorable tax result.

Ordinary Income may be preferable on occasion.

Ordinary income is preferable if you have ordinary losses or deductions items that can be used to reduce your taxable income. Your personal situation may also dictate a need for ordinary income earnings.

Accelerating or Deferring Ordinary Income

The main strategies to accelerate or defer ordinary income focus on the timing of investment purchases and sales. Retirement strategies also provide opportunities to defer or generate ordinary income.

How is ordinary income taxed?

Ordinary income is taxed at ordinary income tax rates. These rates depend on your filing status and the amount of your taxable income.

Ordinary Tax Rates and Filing Status

In order to ascertain the tax rate applicable to your ordinary income, you must first know your filing status.

Marginal Tax Rates

A tax bracket expresses the income tax rate for a given range of income. Ordinary income tax rates are progressive. In other words, the tax rate increases on successively greater earnings. Tax brackets measure this progressive tax structure. The marginal tax rate expresses your rate of tax on your next dollar of income. Currently, the top marginal tax rate for ordinary income is 35 percent. Your effective rate of tax may be greater or less than your marginal rate, depending on the availability of certain losses and deductions. In any event, the marginal rate can provide a quick measure of the tax cost of your investment earnings.

Effective Tax Rates

The effective tax rate measures your actual tax liability as a percentage of your taxable income. In other words, this measures what you actually pay in taxes after considering disallowed deductions or losses. When your taxable income exceeds your true economic income, the effective tax rate is greater than your marginal tax rate. This provides the best measure of the tax cost of your investment earnings.

ABOUT THE AUTHORS

Marcus Ortega and Anthony Williams, founders of Mosaic Financial Associates, have a combined 40 years of experience helping individuals plan, grow, protect, and distribute their net worth with an emphasis on tax planning and asset protection. Their partnership was formed over sixteen years ago culminating with the decision to fulfill their dream of founding their own truly independent holistic wealth management firm. Anthony and Marc's team approach has provided a comprehensive strategy for doctors and their families motivated to achieve their unique financial goals. Some of the concepts with which we assist clients include:

- **Wealth Accumulation**
- **Asset Protection**
- **Tax Minimization**
- **Insurance Strategies**
- **Retirement Distribution Planning**
- **Debt Management**

"Each client is uniquely important to us. The relationships we develop are long-term and mutually beneficial. We believe that balance is imperative in people's personal and financial life and our impact extends beyond our clients' financial success. We aim to provide our clients with a vision, and become their trusted advisor and coach throughout their lifelong financial journey."

Anthony C. Williams, ChFC, CLU, RFC
President, Mosaic Financial Associates

office (480) 776-5920
mobile (602) 770-5948
fax (480) 776-5925
e-mail anthony@mosaicfa.com
website www.MosaicFA.com

Anthony is a Chartered Financial Consultant (ChFC), Chartered Life Underwriter (CLU), and Registered Financial Consultant (RFC). He is a featured keynote speaker on issues pertinent to specialist groups and teaching hospitals throughout the West. He is a graduate of the Arizona State University Business School. He serves in many capacities with Stepping Stones of Hope; a non-profit organization assisting children and their families experiencing the death of a loved one. He is a past board member of SSOH and current Camp Director for Camp Erin, and a volunteer for Camp Paz. He enjoys walking and hiking, traveling, and going to Rocky Point with his wife Wendy, a registered nurse, and his Weimaraner, Tempest.

Marcus E. Ortega, ChFC, RFC
Chief Executive Officer, Mosaic Financial Associates
office (480) 776-5920
mobile (480) 221-5655
fax (480) 776-5925
e-mail marc@mosaicfa.com

Marc is a Chartered Financial Consultant (ChFC), and Registered Financial Consultant (RFC). He graduated from Northern Arizona University with a degree in Finance. Marc began his career in 1994 in Phoenix, Arizona. In January 2008, he co-founded Mosaic Financial Associates, LLC with his long-time business partner, Anthony Williams. He lives with his wife, Dee, and his children Jayden and Marcus. As a family, they love spending time together in Northern Arizona fishing, hiking, and exploring.

CONTRIBUTING AUTHORS

Ike Devji, J.D—Executive Vice President, The Wealthy 100
Of-Counsel, Lodmell & Lodmell, P.C.

Asset Protection attorney Ike Devji was recently named one of only 24 "Leading Wealth and Legal Advisors" in the country by Worth Magazine and his article "Asset Protection 101" has been selected to be honored and presented by the Academy of Financial Services at their annual meeting this fall.

Ike is the Executive V.P of The Wealthy 100 ™, a Phoenix based wealth management and wealth strategy firm with a network of advisors across the U.S. Before joining The Wealthy 100, Mr. Devji, a litigator by training, acted as the Managing Attorney of the law firm of Lodmell & Lodmell, one of the nation's leading Asset Protection only law firms, with a client base of over 3,500 clients and over $5.2 billion in protected assets. Much of the work he does is with and through other professional advisors for their clients.

Mr. Devji currently maintains an of-counsel relationship with the firm and selectively consults and provides Asset Protection services to high-net worth, high liability clients including business owners, developers, C-level executives and professional athletes and entertainers. Ike has spoken on Asset Protection to literally thousands of physicians and other high-net worth clients across the country. He continues to teach continuing legal education on this subject to other attorneys and regularly lectures at the request of leading medical practice management and investment management groups including most recently, MultiFinancial Securities, Greenbook Financial, ING, ING TRUST, Comprehensive Wealth Management, CFO Advisors, numerous banks, and both Lorman and the National Business Institute.

Mr. Devji also consults on a number of other wealth and estate preservation and maximization strategies for qualified individuals including premium financing, real estate depreciation and income and receivables protection strategies.

Ike Devji may be reached at The Wealthy 100 at (602) 808-5540, or by email at ID@thewealthy100.com.

Gary Blume, J.D.—Founder, Blume Law Firm, P.C.

Gary Blume is an experienced attorney with more than 19 years of experience in corporate and business matters. He specializes in contract review. He has provided corporate counsel for many companies for years and has provided planning and strategic advice of not only a legal, but of a business and technical nature. Gary is founder of the Blume Law Firm, PC.

Gary Blume may be reached at Blume Law Firm at (602) 494-7976, or by email at gblume@blumelawfirm.com.

Edwards Brothers Malloy
Oxnard, CA USA
February 4, 2016